The Autism Answer

Finding The Compass Through The Current Of Chaos And Destructive Paths

By

Dr. Frank Lawlis

The Autism Answer

Published in the United States of America

Published By www.MindBodyPlan.com

The Autism Answer
Finding The Compass Through The Current of Chaos

Illustrated by: Alisha Ard

www.Youthapeidia.com

Warning–Disclosure:

Table of Contents

The Autism Answer

Preface

There are many reasons why I felt compelled to write this guide for parents of children diagnosed with autism. One of the greatest needs parents have is for guidance in this oftentimes confusing landscape. Parents have called me for seemingly simple requests – for instance, what to do for their child when they are in a state of bewilderment or fear. Their anxiety, coupled with the needs of their children, has inspired me to embark on this journey.

Parents who have children with autism see their homes destroyed and their dream plans put on permanent hold. Instead of goals and victories, they find themselves living a life of torment and guilt. The related feelings of shame, anger and depression quickly follow the initial denial, and their particular challenge is understood by few.

I seek to put many of these fears to rest. I want to assure you that you can achieve success by using creativity and keeping high spirits. I agree that it is a life that will include much soul searching and exploration, but it will also be a fulfilling life. This experience will ultimately enrich your sense of life's meaning. I cannot tell you the reason why you have been chosen for this life-mission, but here you are and we're going to help you make the very best of it!

I also highly recommend the audio programs we have created that are designed to help your child achieve his or her milestones and goals. Please go to

The Autism Answer

www.MindBodySeries.com/autism   for   more information.

In Gratitude

Many thanks go to Anthony Haskins, Gregory Palumbo and Jim Christopoulos, for their editing and good natured insights, to Wade Younger, for his generous spirit and heart, to Dr. Barbara Peavey, for her wisdom and support, and to Dr. Susan Franks, my wife, for her love and consideration.

The Autism Answer

Part I

Understanding the Autistic Brain

My first goal is to help you understand why your child is behaving the way he or she is, from the perspective of the autistic brain. Brain mapping and neurological portrayals of the autistic brain are very recent in today's autism assessment "toolkit". This kind of "brain imaging" can give you a glimpse of "why" the various "autistic" behaviors may be occurring. It also gives you a deeper understanding of the struggles your child is going through just to look normal – and the great courage they have. But take heart! All of these challenges can be resolved. Nothing is permanent.

Not one of these "autistic" behaviors and traits is necessarily permanent. The brain is a magical organ that has as its primary mission to make life meaningful and joyous. And your brain IS trainable.

Although we will at times get a little (just a little – I promise) technical, keep in mind that this book is not about having to understand all the science and complexities of autism, rather it is about gaining a deeper of understanding of your child and how best to assist him or her.

The Autism Answer

Part II

Psychological Reactions and Adjustment

The psychological community reminds us that not all autistic kids are alike in personality or aptitudes. Moreover, we have to know and understand our triggers that work against us by disrupting the learning and growing process. Once we snap, anxiety overwhelms us, and the situation escalates. Usually, we become overwhelmed by panic – the long-term panic of whether our child will ever be "normal" or the situational panic of whether you will be able to finish dinner at your favorite restaurant. Regardless of the challenge at hand, panic is a deal breaker for education or understanding.

We also need to understand the style by which the child learns best. Like other "atypical" kids, children with autism have their own unique way of understanding, learning and progressing. Some require concrete steps and guidance while others are predisposed to excel using logic.

The Autism Answer

Part III

The Family Dynamics

The most often noted symptom of autism is regressed social skills, even to the point of avoidance of any interactions. Being the most complicated of all acquired proficiencies, social skills are usually observable at the two-year-old range when social dynamics and self identification become magnified. In most cases this is the time-frame when parents and teachers meet the delays and problems head on. Neurological and psychological dimensions are addressed before social interaction is addressed, which from a developmental perspective is the final stage to be dealt with.

The Autism Answer

Part I

Chapter One

An Open Letter to My Family

In the maze of fog and uncertainty that comes along with having a child like me, one of those strange little people with autism, let me tell you what it is like on the other side of this curtain that separates us, you as a parent and me as me. Too often things escalate quickly to crisis mode and only the problems receive your attention; so all you see of me are problems, problems and more problems.

OK, granted I have problems. I have pretty significant problems that affect everything about our relationship, but I am much more than the sum total of the challenges I face. If you are diagnosed with cancer, schizophrenia, diabetes or some other serious illness, you would still be a person, and not just the disease. You would be a multi-dimensional person, full of potential for other aspects of life. Having the disease would only be one facet of your overall being. This is the same for me. I may have a terrible time growing up within the confines of my limitations, but I am more than my limitations.

Give me a break - I am in my developmental phase of my life, and I have much to learn in order to express myself. I am a special person with feelings and I care just like any other person, so don't write me off as "an autistic kid" with limited boundaries. Please know that more than anything I want your love and appreciation. I am like any other kid who wants to grow up, please his parents and know that he is worthy of their love.

I want and need many things from you, perhaps even more than an "ordinary" kid. But please look further than our problems so that I can feel your affection instead of your pain. So often I feel your torment and shame. I can hear it in your voice. I overhear it when you talk with others. I am especially aware of it through your words and actions, and how disappointed you are with what you produced. I watch you look at one another as you lose hope in leading a normal life, all because of me. Please listen to these words as carefully as you can, as I do NOT want your sympathy or pity. It will only limit me and undermine my self assurance, self confidence and belief in myself.

By the very nature of being a child, I am struggling to understand this world in which I was born. It may be frustrating for you, but each day and night is a life-or-death ordeal for me. I am strictly in survivor mode. You may fear the long term consequences of my life; however, I feel fear incessantly in every fiber of my being.

My sensory perceptions are disordered.

For whatever reason, my brain rhythms are not timed right. This is like an automobile motor in which the timing is off. The sparkplugs don't fire ... the carburetor is not adjusted. My auditory system is out

The Autism Answer

of timing as well. It is not that I cannot hear; it is that the words I hear are being decoded at a much slower than normal rate; therefore it takes more time for me to figure out exactly what you are trying to tell me. By the time you move on to another sentence I am still on the first three words of the last one.

And I get very easily by other sounds because I cannot filter them very well. It is not that I am stupid; it is that the timing is confused in my brain. I then get overwhelmed and stressed by all the chaos I am trying so very hard to make sense of.

But the biggest challenge of all is my vision. I can usually "see" what you want me to see, but it is out of context with the rest of the world. If you ask me to look at a ball, I can see the ball, but I can't tell where it is in space. I can't look at your face without getting disoriented. To me, you are floating around in space. I get lost when I try to shift my focus from one thing to another. So in order for me to keep my world in some kind of context, I have to keep everything in as small a space as possible. It may be that I can only look at you out of the corner of my eye if you hold very still. Perhaps I only look at things I can touch and that will not move. I have to be very careful or I feel like I may actually fall into outer space!

Ninety percent of what I can learn is from my visual cues, so maybe you can understand why I am so overly cautious about venturing out and exploring or why any change in routine is so frightening to me. I need to find my own ways to keep the information straight and consistent. I know this is a challenge for you, but imagine how difficult it can be for me.

The Autism Answer

Social Interactions Puzzle Me

If you really want to baffle me, just try to communicate with me in a socially sophisticated way. You will see me run for cover. I get frustrated very easily when attempting to communicate and shut down because of the delays in processing my senses. What I will try to do, if I have everything else under control, is to find a way to respond to you so that you will be happy. Like I said, I am not stupid. So, if you have patience and give me enough time I will find the things that work, at least for me. These things may look like rituals to you, but they are how I have learned to behave in order to feel safe and to provide responses that are as close to normal as possible – all while maintaining control of myself. I will repeat a lot of things and behaviors because they simply work best for me.

To you, my social actions and reactions probably look like crazy behaviors, but they are not. However, when I am in a panic, my actions may very well become "crazy". For the most part this is my way of finding a fixed solution to the complex framework of social interactions which I have yet to make sense of. I don't trust my emotions, and I do not know what yours mean; so I have created these fixed reactions that appear to satisfy you. At least you leave me alone.

The Autism Answer

I Am So Scared

With so much happening that severely distorts my reality, one of my biggest requests is for you to know that most of the time I am scared to death. I keep trying to remind you that I am not dumb because you do not seem to notice how hard I am trying and I get frustrated with the very little reinforcement I receive.

It is when I get scared that I frighten you so much, and I frighten myself as well. If you understand that there are two basic reactions to overwhelming stresses, you may have a deeper awareness of why I am acting the way I do. Stress causes the "fight or flight response". When I experience frustration, I either become combative with anyone in my vicinity, or I withdraw into depression.

When I am out of control and having a meltdown I may inadvertently hurt you or someone else. I have limited skills in stress management, and these will be things I must learn in time. Since my tolerance is very fragile, I know it will be hard for you, but please don't give up on me. There are things I cannot do yet, so please focus on my strengths.

My main request is this: Please understand that although my behavior may be unusual, I want more than anything to please you. I have special strengths of love and intelligence, even though they are hidden from you. And I am still part of you. I am more like you than unlike you, if you can believe it. I have the capacity to make a difference in the world and to you, but it will take time and patience. The faster we can connect to each other, the faster I can prove myself to you.

I am constantly working to find those special ways to orient myself in this world and to get my timing right. I need to develop as many ways as possible to achieve that breakthrough in orientation and timing. Music, light, careful timing and instruction will all be appreciated, but most of all, I need your faith.

With love and appreciation,

Your Child with Autism

Beginning the Journey to Understanding as a Family

I want you to know that I do understand how hard it is for you to maneuver your way through the chaotic and confusing course of life in order to connect to your child with autism and meet his or her requests in meaningful ways. And there are simple facts as to why this understanding has been so fragmented.

I can only imagine the devastation you feel as a mother or father who is seemingly unable to nurture your child, only receiving rebuffs or outbursts of uncontrolled anger when approaching him or her. I have seen hundreds of parents completely overwhelmed by the prospect of raising a child with whom they dread their next interaction - parents who feel an overwhelming sense of shame for bringing such a being into the world. Parents who experience a devastating humiliation that comes from feeling they are unfit to parent a child with autism. Up until now, you have had little or no guidance as to what to do. You have only had hope that wisdom would be gained along the way.

The internet, with all of its strengths and weaknesses, has been the parents' only tool for guidance. Its strength is that people find out they are not alone; however, its weakness is that there is no feasible way to filter through the massive amount of information you will find there. You are left to wonder what or who to trust and believe.

I monitor some of the chat rooms on the web - and even as a practitioner who has spent much of his professional career promoting health, increased inclusion of dietary supplements, and alternative medicine, I am shocked at how many supplements and invasive treatments are recommended for children less than five years of age (like charcoal, IVIG, and a drug to lower testosterone production to name a few).

As a parent in this situation, you might feel like you have no place else to turn. Celebrities become the "experts" based only on their experience as another struggling parent looking for answers. Although much has been published with true altruistic intentions, these are mostly biased and subjective views that could very well be counterproductive – and in some cases they may even possibly endanger your child.

The Autism Answer

Parents Need Help Too

Autism goes much deeper than one child's problem. It affects the entire household and without proper guidance, it becomes a family disaster. There is no surprise that the divorce rate among parents of children with autism is 85%. Divorce consistently emerges as strain and stress eat away at the core of a marital relationship. No one offers guidance for the upkeep of family bonds, and even the healthiest of relationships can be defeated without consistent nurturing and understanding.

Too often, siblings are neglected and do not receive the nurturing necessary to a healthy childhood. They are sometimes thrust into premature adult responsibilities as a result of the focus on the child with autism. This dynamic will usually create even greater stress on the members of the family. Losing their childhood innocence and not building appropriate self reliance skills causes depression to become a chronic threat to the siblings of a child with autism. Such neglect can negatively affect the joys of the human spirit, often lasting a lifetime.

As expressed, this is a guide for the parents (and teachers) of the child with autism; therefore, the guide would not be complete without helping families meet their own needs as well. Without such assistance, the mission of this book would be defeated. Exercises and explanations are included in order to integrate the assessment phase with integrative interventions for the family.

The Autism Answer

The Marking of a Pathway

"**M**arking a path" comes from early pioneer days when paths were explored through forests. The directions of the pathway were indicated by notches cut out of the tree trunks made by earlier scouts in order to "mark" the passage. In that same spirit, this book may serve as the "marks" through the forest of understanding the challenges of having a child with autism and what those challenges mean in the context of everyday life.

The truth is that there are objective measures and definitive guidance available. The research in brain mapping and metabolism gives clarity to the understanding of what is going on at the neuron level. Clearer understanding of how the brain can lack the ability to transmit across regions of varying function reveals how the brain of a child with autism can be trained to function more effectively. The brain may also be "starving" because of an inadequate metabolism, which potentially can be remedied with natural supplements and vitamins.

Vision disorientation has been identified as a very significant problem for children with autism. This may also be trained to function more effectively, increasing proactive and constructive behaviors in these children.

More good news that has recently emerged is the awareness that autism is probably not one but as many as seven or more different syndromes. This helps eliminate the confusion in assessing the wide variety of cases and encourages treatment plans that are tailored to the individual. When this complex disorder is broken down into definable problems that can be measured, it can be treated with specific techniques. This means that very different methods with widely varying characteristics have the same potential for success in terms of creating positive results in your child. In short, there is hope.

The Plan to Discover the Path to Your Child

The design of this book is to "mark the pathway" for understanding your child with autism and to create a process for development toward health. It will provide a step-by-step approach that includes the information you need in order to gage the progress of your child. This will be achieved through a defined course of action that will bring you clarity as to your child's specific strengths. It will also help you define the challenges which need to be addressed in a logical developmental order. Specific treatments will be discussed to bring about noticeable results. Moreover, this guide will give you practical methods to use at home to enhance your child's progress while helping you discover the wonderful child that you know is inside.

The Autism Answer

First of all, what is Autism?

Autism is the fastest growing disability on the planet. What was once a relatively rare condition just 30 years ago, now affects (according to the latest government statistics) at least 1 in 150 children in the United States. It appears that this increase is tracking similarly in most other countries around the world as well.

In 1974 Autism was defined in the DSM I as Childhood Schizophrenia. In 1994 it became defined as Autism Spectrum Disorder - a complex matrix of signs and behaviors. This means that it has been a mere 13 years since any clinical understanding of Autism has been available by virtue of research conducted in a contemporary perspective or method. We have truly been in the dark ages when attempting a dialogue with respect to this very complicated set of disorders. In addition to the lack of understanding among the professionals, even the latest literature admits that "no accurate biological measurement" is being used, and clinical judgment is the "gold standard" of assessment as of this writing.

The Autism Answer

The Mental Health Professionals Point of View

A ccording to the current perspective prevailing within the mental health profession, there is a "formula" for diagnosing autism. This formula is set forth by the DSM IV, which is the diagnostic "bible" that is used by all mental health professionals. Instead of belaboring you with the technical definitions, allow me to lay it out in the words that make the most sense to me. The latest information is that the next version of the DSM (DSM-V) promises to provide a broader definition of autism which will be more parent-friendly for the purposes of insurance coverage, but for the moment, mental health professionals are basing their understanding and diagnosis on the following.

- Major challenges in forming social interactions with others.
- Definite problems in the development of spoken language that is understandable to others.
- Preoccupation with parts of his or her body.
- Slow development in symbolic or imaginative play.
- Unusual repetitive motor activity, such as rocking.

In this guide, we will provide an understanding of how to create a "road map" to find your way through the seemingly overwhelming obstacles that come with having a child with autism. We will review the three fundamental elements that comprise a person's

The Autism Answer

behavioral constitution: Brain Health, Psychological Health and Social Health. The brain health assessment portion is based on the core concept that in order for any individual to learn effectively, the brain has to be in good shape. Using the automobile as a metaphor, if the engine is not running or the wheels are not mounted, it makes no difference what you put in the gas tank - you are going to be frustrated if you try to drive somewhere. You must create a nurturing developmental start by understanding the areas of neurological functioning that need assistance.

This guide is divided into three parts: assessments that determine how the brain is functioning, assessments that determine how the child is functioning and adjusting to brain or psychological reactions, and an assessment of the family's interactions to better manage those dynamics.

Reference Sources
Bailey, A., Phillips, W. & Rutter, M. (1996) Autism: Towards an integration of clinical, genetic, neuropsychological, and neurobiological perspectives. Journal of Child Psychology and Psychiatry and Allied Disciplines, 37 (1), 89 – 126

Carter, A.S., Davis, N.O., Klin, A. & Volkmar, F.R., (2005) Social Development in autism. In F.R. Volkmar, A. Klin, R. Paul & J. Cohen (Eds.) Handbook of Autism and pervasive Developmental Disorders (3rd Edition, Vol. 1), pp. 312-334
Grandin, Temple, The Way I See It (2008) Future Horizons:Arlington, Texas

Chapter Two

The Brain Assessment

O ne of the first steps in the "treatment" journey for your child, is to take a look at what the brain of the child with autism is doing or not doing. In beginning this discussion, it must be pointed out that we now know that the brain has plasticity, meaning that it is flexible and capable of making changes within itself. Naturally, the brain is always changing according to how it is used. The metaphor I use is that of an electrical switch board in which wires that connect one system to another run throughout. These electrical wires are called "neurons" and the average person has about 200 billion of them, all in a 3 pound organ inside your head.

To be truthful, much of the brain remains a mystery and it is still far beyond current human knowledge to fully understand. However, within the last ten years we have made great progress in learning new methods to create changes in the brain. The real magic is that the brain has many backup systems and it is extremely creative in the manners by which it manages its internal connections. For example, people who have permanent brain damage to specific areas of the brain that are responsible for certain functions can re-learn those functions by utilizing other areas of the brain. People who cannot talk are able to learn to talk again. People who cannot walk are able to learn to walk again. Scientists have observed that the brain can "rewire" itself to bring about rehabilitation.

It is with this understanding of brain plasticity that you can take comfort in the knowledge that change can occur within the brain to make one more functional. This is the reason why we need to understand what to change and what are the possible exercises and treatments that will create the desired changes. It is why brain mapping is one of the first steps we usually take because it provides visual confirmation of the problematic brain functions. However, there are other ways aside from brain mapping that will reveal those problematic brain functions as well, and we will investigate these methods.

What Brain Mapping is

The types of brain mapping vary, but the type I use at my clinic (The PsychoNeuroPlasticity Center or "PNP Center") is called a Q-Electroencephalogram or QEEG. This equipment reveals activity levels in various areas of the brain by measuring the electromagnetic frequencies emitted by the brain. The measurements are taken by using electrodes attached to the patients head. There is no pain involved and the procedure is completely non invasive. The patient feels nothing more than the feeling of the electrodes on his or her head. This kind of brain map measures the outside layer or "cortex" of the brain. Other brain maps, such as SPECT and MRIs measure brain function, especially in deeper areas, by looking at the areas of the brain that are using more or

The Autism Answer

less blood. Any of these three types of brain mapping techniques may be used to get a glimpse into what types of activity are occurring in your child's brain.

What We Look For

In autism, there are four patterns that we usually see in children and adults who demonstrate autistic symptoms. The first and most prominent is the lack of coherence or lack of communication between parts of the brain. This means that the frontal lobe may not know what is going on in the temporal lobe and so forth. Like the old saying goes, the left hand doesn't know what the right hand is doing. So it makes sense that children with autism react the way they do. A second pattern we look for is the Mu frequency in the motor strip of the brain which controls the ability to imitate behavior by observing others. The third marker we look at is called the "sinusoidal" frequency. This is the part of the brain located in the front of the head that may be disrupting the ability of the person to pay attention. The fourth and final part of the brain we look at is the back of the brain. This is where we see poor sensory integration, exhibited by a lower frequency which indicates that the senses are not communicating with each other properly. This is so often the case. All of these patterns can show up in any combination, so each person requires a specialized plan.

The Autism Answer

The Four Patterns

1. Coherence

The primary pattern for autism is the lack of "coherence" or the disconnect between the parts of the brain generally responsible for emotional development and structure. Consequently we have major chaos in how effective the brain is at communicating amongst its various regions. Below, you can see how the normal brain functions as compared to the autistic brain when measuring coherence across the different areas, as revealed by EEG brain mapping.

The Autism Answer

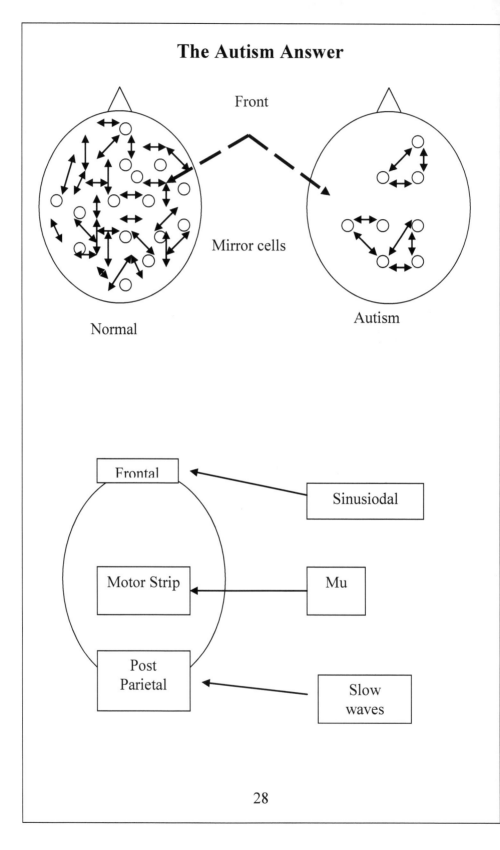

2. The Mu Form

There exist brain cell frequencies that we call the "Mu" form that regulate the flow of information. This Mu pattern is common to most of us, but people with autistic symptoms tend to not be able to regulate this wave and therefore their brains do not allow information to flow effectively. The Mu wave form looks like the Greek letter mu (μ) that has a kind of "cup" pattern that repeats:

Mu wave form

Doctors and scientists have recognized that the Mu form essentially acts a barrier to communication between the different areas of the brain of people exhibiting autistic symptoms.

3. Mirror Cells

We have also discovered that there are cells in the brain referred to as "mirror cells" located in the motor region just off center, 2 to 3 inches over the ears. We call them "mirror cells" because they enable us to mirror or copy someone else's behavior. These are critical to one's ability to learn vicariously. In fact, most of our social learning is accomplished by observing how other people behave and the repercussions of their behavior.

The Autism Answer

If you have ever observed how kids behave after they have seen an exciting movie, you know what I am speaking of, especially if the behavior they observed was aggressive and violent. These mirror cells in the brain of someone showing autistic symptoms are usually either shut down or completely isolated, meaning they are not communicating with other portions of the brain.

Interestingly, in lab experiments, when a rat's mirror cells are destroyed, they no longer act like the other rats. They never mate and often become outcasts. The same is true for people who have a brain injury that affects this area - they also have extreme difficulty in learning new behaviors and adapting to social situations.

4. "Sinusoidal Pattern

We are usually interested in the "sinusoidal" pattern, specifically located in the frontal region of the brain where information is focused upon and organized. The typical pattern is one of a steady flow of information processing, which can be seen in a brain mapping as having low Beta wave frequency (the frequency our brains emit when we are engaged in ordinary daily decisions and activities). However, it is common for the wave form to transform to a Theta wave in children with autism after a short period of time ranging from a few to several minutes. At this point information is no longer recognized.

The Autism Answer

The behavior that is associated with this wave form alteration is observed when a person who is listening and attending to another person suddenly appears to go into a disassociated state or is distracted by a completely different topic or object. This "disconnect" that takes place is often confused with Attention Deficit Disorder.

The Autism Answer

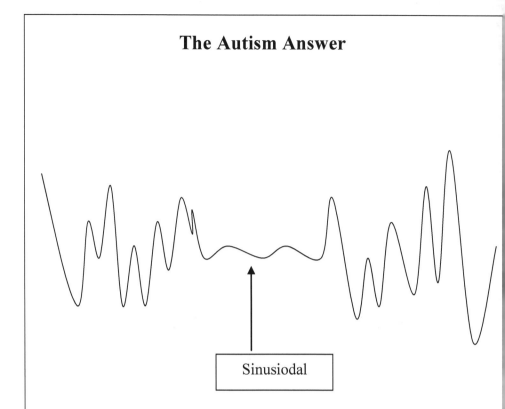

Sinusiodal

The slow brainwave patterns in the back of the brain relate to how well the different sensory inputs are coordinated with each other and within themselves. For example, many autistic children have vision problems, which we shall discuss later in detail. They may be overly sensitive to light or colors. They may not be able to see the background around an object or the person they are attempting to focus upon and therefore become disoriented. Their eyes may not move in coordinated ways. They may be overtly sensitive to sounds as well.

These challenges can amass to become significant obstacles when the child is attempting to orient himself to his environment, and this causes the child major anxiety and stress.

The Autism Answer

Disorders consistent with these Brain map patterns

The following disorders are consistent with the brain map patters we just discussed:

- Autism
- Mental Retardation
- Expressive language disorder
- Asperger's Disorder
- Attention Deficit / Hyperactive Disorder
- Conduct disorder

Audit for behaviors relating to autistic brain mapping patterns

Check off any behaviors described below in order to determine if you or someone you know might be experiencing the "stress storm" patterns associated with autism. "Stress storms" are essentially severe episodes of anxiety.

1. There is impairment to social interactions when the person has to rely on nonverbal cues, such as facial expressions. ( )
2. There is noted difficulty in understanding body postures in the emotions of another. ( )
3. There are strains in conducting interactive communications. ( )
4. There is a lack of social reciprocity when given compliments or support. ( )
5. There is a delay in development of appropriate language, especially when expressing emotions. ( )

6. There is a delay in adequate initiation or the sustaining of conversation. ( )
7. There is inappropriate and spontaneous play behavior. ( )
8. There is a very high and inflexible need for routine. ( )
9. There is a preoccupation with parts of the body. ( )
10. There is poor judgment in predicting what other people might do, if asked in advance. (i.e., what do you think will happen if she smiles at him?) ( )
11. When anxiety and stress mount, there are intentional disruptive behaviors in order to escape the situation. ( )
12. Observable repetitive body movements, such as finger tapping or rocking back and forth. ( )
13. Scoring: If six or more of the observed behavior descriptions are checked, there is a significant implication of the stress storm pattern.

Some Potential Recommended Treatment plans

As these and other brain patterns reveal themselves, remember that I assured you that the brain can be trained and refocused. Some of the best successes have been with creative exercises developed on the heels of the revelations provided by the brain mapping results. The most common recommendations are:

1. Brain Training or Neurotherapy

The most encouraging innovation has come from Michael Linden and the Thompsons with their use of neurotherapy. Neurotherapy is a method of teaching a person to retrain their brain by monitoring their neuroactivity and guiding the person using internal imagery or physiological shaping. For example, this can be done by changing breathing patterns as the person finds ways of structuring their brain function to facilitate constructive goals. It may also be achieved through operant conditioning, in which you gain rewards (social reinforcement, points in a game, etc.) by shaping a response in the brain, such as raising the amplitude of alpha for anxiety training or lowering theta frequencies for ADD.

2. Hyperbaric chamber

This is a very old treatment for deep sea divers who get the "bends" when they surface too quickly, but it has been demonstrated to help the brain heal and develop, especially in the event of strokes or head injury. A hyperbaric chamber is an enclosure within which you lie as air pressure is increased, which forces oxygen into the body and aids in healing. It does not hurt and the patient is even able to watch a movie, read a book or sleep during the treatment.

3. Physical Exercise

Brain function can be improved through exercise as well, especially with coordination exercises. Some of the most beneficial exercises have been ones that involve interactions with other people, such as playing catch or riding a seesaw. The cooperative exercises combined with physical activities play a significant role in developing trust in others as well as increasing brain activities for coherence.

4. Music

Another physical activity that has a profound positive impact is moving rhythmically to music. It is very difficult for a person showing the stress pattern to move gracefully and they often may appear resistant, especially in social settings, but with encouragement he or she can and will participate. It is interesting because children with autism are often observed to be rocking back and forth as a means of relaxation and self stimulation when they are alone, so this kind of activity can be derived from that underlying need for rhythmic motion. We developed The Autism Answer Audio Program available at
www.MindBodySeries.com/Autism, with music specifically "encoded" with audio frequencies and rhythms to help with autism. Visit the website for more information.

5. Direct stimulation of brain regions

We have found that for many of our patients sonic stimulation can provide a jump start to changing brain patterns. For example, by using a device called the BAUD (Bio-Acoustical Utilization Device, which can be purchased through The PNP Center) the brain's regions may be retrained to more constructive patterns, such as the slowing in the back of the brain. A more consistent pattern may be maintained as well, such as the sinusoidal wave form.

The Autism Answer

Manny, A Child with Autism

Even at the age of four, Manny showed the behavior patterns of autism. To most of his family members he seemed like a feisty child with a very high intelligence and an aptitude for problem solving. But his mother felt a major lack in the kind of bonding that she experienced with her older children. Manny never wanted to be cuddled or nurtured in any way. He rejected any attempts to teach him how to socialize with other children and continually isolated himself from groups, always preferring to be alone. His mother also thought it was odd that he didn't appear to be jealous of the other children who did receive attention.

Manny struggled with social relationships, finding it difficult, even impossible, to behave under any structure. Sometimes he would hurt other children because of his self-centered needs, such as pushing other children in order to get what he wanted. When he would become frustrated, he would scream or grunt while he ran around banging his head. All of his strange behaviors were his own inventions. He was subsequently diagnosed with autism.

In an odd way Manny was sensitive to those around him, but he could not interact with anyone. When I began seeing him, it appeared to me that he was trying to make an effort, but there was a sense of disconnection. Although he showed sensitivity to the danger of an angry dog, he could not relate to other children's emotions in this way. He had no empathy to how others felt or any inclination to meet their needs.

When Manny was brought to the clinic, a brain scan (QEEG) showed what I had expected see. The communication among the different parts of the brain was limited only to a bare minimum. This was especially true between the frontal and parietal lobes, which control long-term planning and spatial sense and navigation. Moreover, the nerve cells responsible for learning by imitating behaviors in the parietal lobe were not working effectively. The combination of these limitations might explain why Manny could not learn social skills from others, as well as why he was unable to organize the signals of his senses, like sight and sound, into meaningful understandings. It also made perfect sense that without the integration of sensory input, any touch or interaction from others seemed startling and confusing.

In just a year, Manny has shown significant advances in the way he relates to the world. He is still participating in a neurotherapy program where the goal has been to reconnect the different parts of his brain so that his "timing" and sensory communication is like that of most kids. What we did for Manny is to teach him and his family techniques they could use to train the frontal lobe to relax enough in order to begin to process things more easily and slowly without anxiety and stress getting in the way.

The Autism Answer

As Manny was going through this brain re-training, he continued his behavioral training to learn social conventions and appropriate ways to get the things he wants while demonstrating sensitivity to others. He also discovered some insights on his own which helped him a great deal. As he gained access to the outer world, his depression lifted and he started a major thrust toward interaction, even getting a girlfriend and two buddies that he enjoyed spending time with.

Manny started his plan from ground zero. Nothing had helped significantly before, and we always worry about how eager someone like Manny will be in trying new techniques after so many dead-ends. Throughout his treatment plan, we did not deceive ourselves into thinking that he was cured and that everything would progress automatically into normalcy. But we built a bridge for him to use and we had faith that as his constructive stress management tools were employed, they would become stronger. We were very optimistic about that.

The Autism Answer

Summary Thoughts

The autistic brain pattern is by definition a very complicated interactive and seemingly chaotic picture, and is perhaps the most complex array of different dynamics of all the mental disorders. This is largely due to the immaturity of children with whom we see these problems – they are so young that they have little or no ability to speak for themselves, and there is a decided lack of technology available to understand psychological manifestations directly from the brain. In support of the latter point, we have been using the DSM, the accepted diagnostic guide for psychologists and psychiatrists for the last twenty years, which only has a handful of scientific technologies recommended to differentiate categories of pathological mental functioning. The primary use of the interview form of evaluation is the least reliable of all forms for diagnoses and therefore it can be extremely difficult for parents to develop a functional plan.

In summary, autism is a challenge that requires patience and time, but I am optimistic about the future as science makes consistent breakthroughs in this area. I have watched individuals, like Manny, whose behavioral patterns were seen as so bizarre that he was given up for adoption to the state because his parents were overwhelmed with hopelessness. I have been fortunate to see many Mannys and their progression, lending to the optimistic perspective I entertain. However, I can also grieve for the thousands of families who have not been privy to the resources available and are caught in a quagmire of horror, depression and the many challenges they face. But please understand that there is hope. The knowledge of how the autistic brain functions can bring you much needed insight and understanding into what your child with autism may be experiencing at the brain level. This affords you the opportunity to tailor your interactions with your child in a more understanding and patient fashion. If you would like to have a brain mapping of your child with autism, contact your local physician.

Reference Sources

Doidge, N., (2007) The Brain that Changes Itself, Viking: New York
Rapin, L. & Katzman, R. (1998) Neurobiology of autism. Annals of Neurology, 43 (1), 7-14

Chapter Three

Visual Competencies

Because children process information through their visual sensory system 90 percent of the time, it is obvious that if that system is not coordinated properly, they will be disoriented to their world. Moreover, they will be fearful to explore their world and even looking at others to study their facial expressions may cause emotional pain.

Suppose your child has a special visual problem that does not allow him to see the field around an object. This is called "ambient vision" where you see the object of interest but you lose orientation of its location in the space surrounding it. By using yoked prisms (which look something like eye-glasses) on these children there may sometimes be instant success. Instead of hugging the wall or isolating themselves, they start exploring their environment like normal children. There are immediate changes from toe-walking to normal, flat walking. There is much better hand-eye coordination, posture in sitting and walking. There is a behavioral shift from hyperactive and inattentive conduct to calm and attentive conduct. Interestingly, this can result in long-term changes, including increased attention span, increased speech abilities, enhanced social skills, and better academic performance. These observations are common in at least 40 percent of children diagnosed with autism who have vision challenges.

The Autism Answer

Now, imagine how it feels to be so completely disoriented that you don't know top from bottom, left from right or where you are in space. You would be frightened out your wits, scared of everything, and you would only trust yourself. Your internal signals are the only things you could locate and understand. And interestingly, children with these challenges have no idea that they have this distortion because this is the only way they have seen and experienced the world.

There are two primary visual problems that a child has to overcome to determine how he will deal with his upside down world. The first is called "tunnel vision" or compressed vision (also known as hyper-converged vision), in which the field of vision is restricted to a relatively small area. Only the elements in that small region can be processed, leaving out the rest of the surroundings.

Imagine that you can see a dog in your tunnel, but you cannot place the dog in relationship to anything else. Your world-view would comprise of two dimensions instead of three, which makes distance judgment impossible. In order to understand your mother talking to you, you must "see" the face and read the emotional messages as well as the verbal content. Not having the connection between object and environment or words and emotions makes it very difficult for the child with autism to correctly understand and interpret the messages he or she receives. After all, 90% of communication is nonverbal. However, a child with autism can focus only on the mouth in order to comprehend the words and therefore loses the many emotional messages that come with the words. In many cases, the world around him will feel as if it is falling in on them, which makes it a very scary place for him.

The second visual problem is "Alternating" vision or "visual disparity". This experience occurs when the eyes see two different images with no overlap. By only seeing two different views of the world, the child has the perception of conflict between two images because the transition from one eye to another is too slow to create continuity. For example, instead of seeing a smooth movement in a movie, the autistic child may only see flickering pictures. If the transition become too fast, which sometimes happens, life will become a blur. This can cause nausea and motion sickness, so the child spends a lot of time learning to suppress their visual torment as a survival instinct that results from the confusing and distressing messages they are receiving from outside them.

The Autism Answer

What behaviors are associated with visual problems?

The following are some behaviors that are related to the visual problems children with autism manifest. Check to see if your child may be exhibiting them.

1. Looking at other people through the corners of their eyes (because monocular vision, or vision using just one eye at a time, is easier to cope with and understand).

2. They cannot look at the people they are conversing with (because they can't process two sources of information at the same time).

3. They often hug walls or try to limit the space they use when walking in their surroundings.

4. They get stressed when you ask them to perform visual tasks.

5. They have problems following moving objects.

6. They wiggle their fingers in front of them in order to gain perspective.

7. They often "spot", which means they fixate on a focus point, moving their head instead of their eyes.

The Autism Answer

8. They like to touch objects or surfaces they are seeing (in order to make sure they are real and not some perceptual trick).

9. They walk with great caution.

10. They have no body boundary sense in space, so they misjudge where they are in relationship with someone else.

11. They cannot play catch and will often become anxious when asked to participate.

12. They hold onto objects (trusting what they can grip and touch), and then lose them in their visual space when the object is released.

13. They toe-walk.

14. They take short steps.

15. They need to feel for the chair that they will be sitting in and once seated, will sit awkwardly.

The Autism Answer

Evaluation

We usually recommend the Kaplan Nonverbal test, but each professional vision specialist may have their own approach. Observing behaviors while the child is asked to perform visual tasks is the primary method of evaluation. For example, the child may be asked to watch a video and is observed as to the manner in which he watches (tilting head, watching with one eye, etc.). He may be asked to perform a task while dealing with other demands, such as balancing to gravitational forces. There may be interaction with the examiner. All of these may be done with the use of yoked ambient prism lens that will help the child see ambients field in much greater detail. What is so exciting is that when the appropriate prisms are used, the child will respond immediately with normal behavior.

What you will be looking for

The richness of the examination provides an immediate outcome in behavior. The child will walk better and communicate more effectively. There will be an immediate curiosity in exploring his or her environment and he or she will show much less stress in doing so. The parent is usually so enthusiastic with this that there is often an impulse to conclude that the child is cured. The news is seldom that good, however, and there must be a plan that includes visual exercises to help develop the right visional strength on a long term basis.

The Autism Answer

Potential recommendations

- Vision therapy, very much like physical therapy for the eyes.
- Prescriptive lenses.
- Multiple sensory integration, such as teaching to listen and coordinating verbal with visional information processing.
- Cranial-sacral physical therapy (to make better balance of muscles.)
- Biofeedback (to learn to de-stress the body and control muscles and mood more effectively.)
- Coordinating breathing and movement with vision tasks.
- Learning to understand body language of others.

In summary, it is worth your time and effort to explore your child's vision cues in order to find exercises that may help him essentially put the world in perspective. Much of this can be done by simple observation. Using the exercises I have discussed, you may find that over time your child with autism can come to a better understanding of the world around him, thereby decreasing their stress and anxiety responses. This will lead to a happier, healthier experience for both you and your child.

Reference Sources

Kaplan, Melvin. Seeing through New Eyes, (2006), Jessica Kingsley: London Grandin, Temple, The Way I See it (2008), Future Horizons: Arlington, Texas

Chapter Four

Brain Toxicities

Although the controversy over exposure to heavy metals, such as mercury, has been in the news as possible causes of autism, only about 13 percent of the children evaluated for autism have shown clinically significant levels. However, many problems in those studies exist with the methodology of the lab work, which we will discuss later. Nevertheless, heavy metal exposures, such as mercury, lead, aluminum, petroleum products, etc. have been specified by the American Psychological Association to be significant contributors to cognitive incapacities. They have been found to be disruptive to a person's ability to think and behave normally.

What is worse is that we have found that these heavy metals have been found in much of the population of people with learning and emotional challenges. These metals are often embedded in the lymph nodes and fatty tissues especially in the brain, and can cause significant brain dysfunction.

Toxicities from the mercury used in vaccines, principally measles, mumps and rubella, have been seriously considered as inducing a cascade of poor auto-immune reactions which produce autistic behaviors. Recent evidence has shown that exposure to heavy metal is the cause for brain dysfunction in a large portion of children who manifest asocial behaviors. What we still do not know is whether the mercury exposure causes the brain problem or whether these particular children lack some enzyme that normally would have metabolized the mercury out of their system, as only a relatively small percentage of children are affected. This is certainly true for the metabolism of copper, which can have the same impact on the brain as mercury.

Another component of toxicities in the brain is the allergies or sensitivities a child manifests which can be directly linked to the cognitive problems related to autism. For example, allergies due to exposure to food or environmental substances have a consequential reaction of an autoimmune attack on some part of the body, usually where heat is highest, since heat is a signal of injury or disease (blood vessel enlargement).

The result is high levels of inflammation, which increases the body's toxicity "alarm" that is triggered by the by-product of the destroyed cells and tissue.

One of the most likely sites for these targeted areas of high heat is the brain, especially if the child has excessive anxiety or worries, which definitely fits the profile of the child with autism. High levels of toxicity can damage the connections between the neurons meaning that communication among different areas of the brain is hindered. Toxicity can lower the activities of certain regions of the brain and burden it with destructive activities. Interestingly, the "cause" of Multiple Sclerosis has often been attributed to this very same process.

The Autism Answer

Allergies and food sensitivities have been attributed to non-constructive and abnormal behavior, and have even been named in the same category of behaviors as autistic. However, the main difference is that these asocial behaviors will dissipate after the digestion process completes. But if the child is regularly subjected to toxic environmental conditions, such as pesticides and/or preservatives which can be found in carpets and linens, he or she may begin to display behavior in these non-constructive and abnormal ways.

Behaviors related to allergies and sensitivities to food and environmental substances

Check off the symptoms your child may show, especially if he has recently been exposed to a food or a toxic environmental situation:

Symptom	Present
Runny nose	( )
Hypersensitive skin	( )
Itchy eyes	( )
Stuffy nose, sneezing	( )
Rapid pulse	( )
Marked behavior change	( )
Increased anxiety or stress	( )
Red ears or cheeks	( )
Mood swings	( )
Stomach ache	( )
Gas and bloating	( )
Constipation or diarrhea	( )
Dark circles under the eyes	( )

The Autism Answer

Rash   ( )
Headaches   ( )
Diminished concentration   ( )
Diminished memory   ( )
Diminished emotional control   ( )
Diminished visual abilities   ( )
Sleep problems   ( )
Diminished appetite   ( )
Sugar cravings   ( )
Symptoms worse on damp days   ( )
The touch of clothes become painful   ( )

If you have checked off more than one symptom, it is time to do a house check for mold, paint, and old or new carpeting for possible chemicals, formaldehyde or other preservatives.

Evaluations

The best step to take when a child is showing these symptoms is to evaluate whether your child has had exposures to these elements. Then we can take steps to eradicate that factor which consequently "cleans up" the brain. There are basically two approaches: direct and indirect.

One direct method is urine samples evaluated by the Genova Lab after two days of oral chelation. Chelation is a term that typically means the cleansing of the body, although it does have a wide array of meanings in the field of medicine. One of the first chelations was a blood cleansing in which the blood was put through a cleansing solution; however it proved to be very dangerous. The process is typified by the administration of a supplement that binds to metallic molecules, making the molecules larger so that they may be extracted, thus cleansing the system of metallic elements. This works in the same way that the molecules in soaps and cleaners attach to particulates in order to cleanse a surface. There are more recent developments; however, and what we use at the PsychoNeuroPlasticity Center (PNP) is an oral chelation agent called DSMA (meso-dimercaptosuccinic acid) in order to bring the metallic elements into the urine and out of your system. I highly recommend carefully selecting a physician who knows what he or she is doing in this regard because this is a process that should be supervised by an experienced physician. We have been doing this at PNP for over six years and have had only one case who "didn't feel well". We immediately discontinued the treatment. We are very cautious and you must be as well.

Subsequent to eradicating heavy metals from the body, we use the test available through Genova labs to determine if there are significant levels remaining. Since the lab test utilizes urine, these tests can be done at home.

The direct evaluation to test the body for heavy metals does not involve a blood test, as many physicians suggest. Since most of these heavy metals and substances exist as fat-soluble substances, they are usually hidden, often undetectable in the lymph glands, and therefore do not show up in blood tests. Hair tests are often recommended because of their residue in hair cells, but these tests have proven unreliable as well.

The indirect method, is to take some action (such as using one of the natural cleansers below) for cleansing and see if the behavior changes. Regardless of what method is used, you have to know what you are dealing with in order to know the path to solving the challenges. It may be necessary for repeated tests to see if progress is being made since many people inadvertently continue to be exposed in their homes, schools or workplace. These nasty compounds can cause a lot of human suffering, and since they are so common, it may be necessary for regular check-ups.

The problem elements we want to eliminate as contributors in your child's brain problems

Examine tables A, B, C and D for some research done regarding the direct impact to cognitive function resulting from exposure to a number of substances commonly found in the home.

The Autism Answer

Table A

Affects of Exposure to Heavy Metals on Cognitive Abilities

Cadium (common from Manufacturing waste)	Motor dysfunction Decreased IQ Hyperactivity Hypoactivity
Lead	Learning difficulties Decreased IQ Impulsivity Attention Deficit Hyperactivity Violence
Manganese	Brain Damage Motor dysfunction Memory impairment Attention Deficit Compulsive Disorder
Mercury	Visual impairment Learning disabilities Attention Deficit Motor dysfunction Memory Impairment Behavioral problems

The Autism Answer

Table B

Affects of Exposure to Solvents on Cognitive Abilities

Ethanol (alcohol)
Learning Difficulties
Attention Deficit
Memory Impairment
Eating / sleeping disorders
Mental retardation

Styrene
Hypoactivity
Lack of Inhibition

Toluene
Learning Disabilities
Speech deficits
Motor dysfunction

Trichloroethylene
Hyperactivity
Lack of Inhibition

Xylene
Motor dysfunction
Learning difficulties
Memory Impairment

The Autism Answer

Table C

Affects of Exposure to Pesticides on Cognitive Abilities

Organochlorines / DDT	Hyperactivity Decreased energy / effort Decreased coordination Memory Impairment
Organophosphates (including DFP, Dursban, diazinon)	Hyperactivity Attentional Disorders Decreased ability to follow instructions
Pyrethroids (including Bioallethrin, deltamethrin, Cypermethrin,)	Hyperactivity Attentional problems

The Environmental Working Group, using data from the USDA and FDA pesticide research bank from 1992 to 1997, have compiled a list of the most contaminated fruits and vegetables available directly to consumers. As a rule of thumb, it is critical and mandatory that all fruits and vegetables be washed and even peeled to reduce exposure to toxic chemicals.

Apples	Grapes (from Chile)
Spinach	Potatoes
Peaches	Red raspberries
Pears	Celery
Strawberries	Green beans

The Autism Answer

Table D

Affects of exposure to other common substances on Cognitive Behavior

Nicotine	Hyperactivity
	Learning disabilities
	Developmental delays
Dioxins	Learning disabilities
PCBs	Learning disabilities
	Attention Deficits
	Hyperactivity
	Memory Impairments
Fluoride	Hyperactivity
	Decreased IQ

Listed below are substances that are natural cleansers of toxins and may be used to evaluate your child's behavior after one or more trials:

Stimulating the Body's Natural Cleansing Enzymes

Additional substances that aid in the detoxification process are:

(Use the published dosages on the labels).

Calcium-D-glucarate – a calcium salt of D-glucaric acid allows for increased net elimination of toxins and steroid hormones.

The Autism Answer

N-acetyl-L-cysteine (NAC) – produces a dramatic acceleration of urinary methylmercury excretion in animals and reduces liver damage.

Alpha-ketoglutarate (AKA) – helps detoxify ammonia, synthesized from urea in the colon, often associated with Rett Syndrome in children. Very effective as an anti-oxidant.

Methyl-sulfonyl (MSM) – a naturally occurring sulfur compound used in detoxification processes.

Taurine – a conditional essential amino acid that appears to inhibit catecholamine oxidation in the brain. Taurine is also required for the formation of bile salts, an important mode of toxin elimination.

Methionine – a sulfur-bearing amino acid found in animal proteins that assist in the removal process for heavy metals as well as aiding in the excretion through the urine.

Choline – acting as a neurotransmitter as well as metabolism enhancer, this ingredient is very important at the cellular level of detoxification.

Betaine anhydrous – also known as trimethylgcine, is a major metabolite of choline. This substance is usually found in small amounts in beets, spinach, and seafood.

Selenium – required for the synthesis for a vital antioxidant enzyme that helps detoxify hydrogen peroxide reproduced within cells.

Modifilan - basically brown seaweed, that was used for stripping radiation from the Chernobyl event in Russia and has since been used to remove heavy metals by the armed forces.

Besides being stimulants for increasing the body's activities, there are some supplements that purportedly do some of the actual cleansing. These are some supplements we recommend at the clinic as additional sources the parents may use in their everyday life:

- P-5-P is a form of vitamin 6: The unique quality of this resource is that it gets past the blood/brain barrier. P5P is the active enzyme form of vitamin B6 that does not require activation by the liver. Its ability to alter the inflammatory concentrations may arise from its important status in the metabolism of these immunity agents. The P5P-containing enzymes and results in the formation of the amino acid cysteine, which is then transformed into inorganic sulfates or taurine, major anti-inflamatory elements.

- Arginine (L-form): One of the 20 most common natural amino acids, Arginine is synthesized from citrulline by the sequential action of the cytosolic enzymes. Citrulline accumulates along with nitrate and nitrite, the stable end-products of NO, in NO-producing cells. Arginine plays an important role in cell division, the healing of wounds, removing ammonia from the body, immune function, and the release of hormones.

- Wobenzym is a German product that is simply a combination of six enzymes that reduce inflammation.

- Coenzyme Q10 (also known as CoQ10) has been used for mood and memory enhancement.

- L-theanine (5-N-ethylglutamine) has been used in instances of trauma or periods of severe stress. These symptoms are prevalent with Aspergers and Autistic Syndromes. This substance has been found in green tea.

- Carnosine is a natural substance that has been used to foster frontal lobe function (increased attention and focus) and has a brain protective function. Individuals with autistic features have been shown to improve in vocabulary and organization.

- The combination of American ginseng (200 mg.) and Ginkgo biloba (50 mg.) has been shown to have significant improvements for hyperactive-impulsive behaviors as well as improving high anxiety – shy traits related to social problems. There has also been improvement in performances of quality of memory at the highest dose and speed of attention at a mid-dose range.

The Autism Answer

American ginseng has been documented to enhance central nervous system activity (brain and spinal cord), decrease fatigue, and increase motor activity. Ginseng has antidepression, antipsychotic, anticonvulsant, analgesic, antipyretic and ulcer-protective qualities. Psychologically it has been shown to inhibit conditioned avoidance responses. Interestingly related to toxicity, it has an anti-inflammatory quality for the brain.

Special Note on detoxification damage

With due respect to all the discussion about the harm that heavy metals and other contaminants can do to the brain and other systems of the body, we have seen many people who simply have damage to their detoxification systems and cannot rid themselves of these elements. For example, one of the heavy metals that has been considered as an explanation for high anxiety and depression has been copper. But what we have found is that the problem is not an over-exposure to copper, but a problem with the detoxification systems that fail and lack the ability to rid the body of excess copper.

The Autism Answer

One interesting question is: do children affected by heavy metals might have damaged detoxification systems. The best way to check for this possibility is a blood test for levels of Gluamine and perhaps N-Acetyl Cysteine. Glutamine is the primary substance that detoxifies the body; if found to be problematic, it should be managed for successful results.

Reference Sources

Lawlis, Frank, The IQ Answer, (2006) Viking: New York
Lawlis, Frank, The ADD Answer, (2004) Viking: New York

Chapter Five

Nutrition and Brain Fuel

During the early eighties I co-founded a new program in psychology called "Behavior Medicine," which is a blend of alternative behavioral approaches to medical problems. One of the methods is a nutritional approach to psychological issues in which we found people who were getting psychologically and biologically sick from the food they ate. We devised an "ecology clinic" in which we could evaluate what foods were causing problems for which patients. We used a very basic procedure of watching what people ate and the behavior they exhibited 30 minutes later. One of these patients was a six-year-old boy named David.

David was labeled as bi-polar because he had wild mood swings. One moment he was a kind and gentle child, the next moment he was a tyrant, kicking the walls and creating havoc. This was a lesson to me as I observed that subsequent to taking three bites of a grapefruit, we witnessed the transition from a cute little boy into a menacing monster. Of course, we discovered that the food was the problem.

The Autism Answer

Autism is not commonly described as a disorder with wide spread emotional mood-swings, but I have learned how the wrong food can make anyone's brain wreak emotional havoc. My own brain goes to sleep when processing sugar and I have to watch any intake whatsoever if I desire to drive home safely.

While it is true that brain dysfunctions have many sources, nutrition is a major consideration. There is brain food; there is brain-drain food; and finally, there is brain-strain food. Different foods can cause huge stresses in your system that can disrupt normal body and mind processes, the quality of your experiences and even interfere with and destroy memory.

Let's say that your child started the day eating jelly doughnuts washed down with orange juice. Remember that their body has been away from food for ten to twelve hours while they slept (hopefully), so you are breaking fast (hence the name breakfast) with huge amounts of sugar into his blood stream. None of our bodies are made to handle that kind of sugar load. Historically, we ate much less sugar, especially processed sugars, than we do today. So, the processed sugars send your child's blood sugar soaring and disrupt the normal function of the kidneys and blood vessels. The body's natural response to this unnatural sugar load is to then produce an excess of insulin.

The Autism Answer

Relative levels in the blood stream

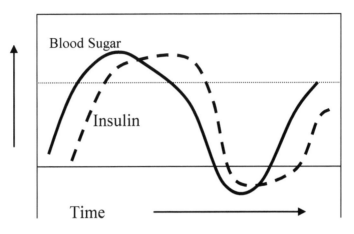

Insulin is the substance that binds with the blood sugar and helps transport it into the organs, muscles and brain for use. Without the help of insulin, the blood sugar would just pool in the blood stream and cause all kinds of problems, which is what happens with diabetes. As you can see from the graph, when you introduce sugar into the system at a high rate, the insulin then pumps from your pancreas at full steam trying to reduce the amount of blood sugar to safe levels. Often, the over-stressed pancreas cannot keep up and so inflammation begins to build.

The Autism Answer

This is not a desirable effect. When the pancreas falls behind in trying to deal with a massive sugar intake, insulin production sets off on a roller-coaster ride for the rest of the day. Just by starting out with a more "natural" meal with a balance of complex carbohydrates and protein, the nature of those foods provides a slower, steadier caloric burn. This provides the body the fuel it needs without overtaxing it. There is no "sugar high" when you eat a balanced meal because there exists an integrated and regulated flow of insulin and blood sugar.

The sugar high triggers huge changes in energy levels and brain power, but twenty minutes after your child eats, the high flow of insulin generated transports the blood sugar to your organs. Any excess insulin produced also wipes out reserve blood sugar, sending the energy and brain systems into a major crash. This is what we call the hypoglycemic response. It is nothing to mess around with. People who are particularly sensitive can even go into comas.

Since the brain does not store sugar but requires more of it than any other organ in the body, it runs out of fuel early during the hypoglycemic response. It doesn't help when your child responds to low blood sugar by dumping more unnatural levels of it into their already messed up system. When he or she stumbles across the room and gulps down another candy bar or high sugar food, they do get another rush, but it is only the beginning of a new roller-coaster ride. At some point, they will have to get off the ride. If you continue to stress your pancreas, it may fail. Then, you are looking at a high probability of diabetes and heart disease, both of which can lead to permanent brain damage.

Besides developing a very big problem by consuming a bad breakfast, there are numerous issues that arise when the body acts as if food is an enemy - as is the case with food allergies or sensitivities. There are many reasons for why the body's immune system learns to react in specific manners to certain foods, such as building up inflammation. For example, your child may have what is called a "leaky gut," which means the grooves in his or her stomach have created wide cracks and the food is spilling through them in ways that the body perceives as a threat. That sets up another situation in which the body begins to reject food when you over-consume. There are documented cases involving the over-consumption of orange juice and milk causes a negative reaction. In medical terms, this form of reaction is considered a "sensitivity" because the immune system only reacts when it receives an "overload" signal, whereas allergies are triggered regardless of the amount of food consumed.

The Autism Answer

Check Your Child Out

To assess whether your child may be reacting to his nutrition efficiently, take the following home evaluation. These items are particularly sensitive to the issue of nutritional imbalance.

1. Are there times in the day when your child has great loss of energy?

2. Does your child crave sugar or sweets during the day?

3. Is your child forgetful, especially in the morning?

4. Does your child usually have a high sugar breakfast and then is hungry the rest of the day?

5. Does your child have major difficulty concentrating 30 minutes after sugar or a specific food?

6. Does your child have trouble falling asleep?

7. Is your child stressed most of the time?

8. Although your child is thirsty, does he or she drink little water each day?

9. Is your child sensitive to medications or supplements?

10. Does your child have irrational fears that have no basis?

11. Does your child have stomachaches and other digestive tract problems, such as constipation or diarrhea?

12. Do your child's joints and muscles ache?

13. Does your child have major mood swings almost every day?

14. Does your child only want or like fried foods, even if there are more nutritious foods available?

15. Is your child's energy limited and does he or she get weak quickly?

Scoring: If you answered yes on more than two items you should consider nutrition as an important part of your child's mental potential and you may be in need of a nutritional consultation in order to prevent a significant delay in their cognitive abilities and development.

Assessment

There are numerous special health care professionals who profess to evaluate your child's nutritional program and possible allergy issues. I have no preferences to recommend, but most will use a food diary as the start. This is the format we follow at The PNP Center. In short, you need to write down what your child eats and record any behavioral changes that occur in the following 30 to 60 minutes.

The Autism Answer

Time	Food Consumed	Behavior Noted
_____	_____	_____
_____	_____	_____
_____	_____	_____
_____	_____	_____
_____	_____	_____
_____	_____	_____
_____	_____	_____
_____	_____	_____
_____	_____	_____
_____	_____	_____
_____	_____	_____
_____	_____	_____
_____	_____	_____
_____	_____	_____

The Autism Answer

If there is a particular food that is identified as possibly problematic, we usually recommend that you suspend that food for ten days. Then with deliberation, you begin to re-introduce that food. If there is a dependency on the food, then the child will crave it and the consequent behavior will be magnified. That is the basic signal to avoid that food. You may find that there may be a group foods, such as milk and cheese, which share a common ingredient, such as dairy. That is the cue to avoid the entire group. The most common groups of problematic foods are dairy, wheat, corn, and sugar cane.

Positive Foods for Brain Power

Rather than scare you into being afraid of food, I need to assure you that many foods have a very positive effect upon the brain. I am recommending the following as potential for increasing your child's brain-power and aiding in its expeditious development. I would use the same method described above to identify the most effective foods for your child.

Water – I realize that this ingredient is not a food per se, although it often comes in a pretty bottle at a steep price. Nevertheless, water deserves respect as a major stimulator for neurotransmission in the brain. While there are obvious differences in water's composition (sources, minerals, etc.), no one kind of water appears to provide an advantage in the development and improvement of intelligence. I'll leave it to your personal preferences when it comes to taste and purity.

I will caution you that tap water in some areas is saturated with fluoride and residual medications that re-enter a community's ground-water source. Traces of many medications are often found, including traces of anti-depressants. I am not against fluoride, but it makes your body absorb aluminum faster, which is one of the most toxic metals commonly associated with brain dysfunction. While many children don't care to consume large quantities of water, there are ways to make it more appealing, such as adding lemon and light quantities of natural juices to help improve its taste.

Natural complex carbohydrates – Natural carbohydrates include whole grains, fruits and vegetables.

Antioxidants – When your child gets exposed to things like alcohol and cigarette smoke, "free radicals" are released. These free-ranging agents keep the body from using oxygen efficiently, which is referred to as oxidation. You can see this reaction in other forms by observing the rust that forms on iron, or the spoiling of food over time. Because the brain consumes more oxygen than any other organ in the body, it is especially vulnerable to oxidation. To protect your brain, you need to consume antioxidants. The chief vitamin antioxidants are vitamin C, vitamin E, vitamin B6 and B12. Others include selenium, zinc, calcium and magnesium.

The Autism Answer

Supplements have been shown to increase various functions, but real food is still the best way to get nutrients. Therefore, I recommend the following foods as major suppliers of antioxidants:

Beets
Red Grapes
Berries, especially blueberries and raspberries
Red peppers
Spinach
Prunes
Citrus fruits
Sweet potatoes
Carrots
Tomatoes
Onions
Broccoli
Asparagus
Cabbage
Brussels sprouts
Beans
Watermelon
Wheat germ
Nuts

Omega-3 fats – These are the super-stars of brain foods. They are more commonly known as fatty acids or "good fats." The term "Omega" refers to the classification of the kind of fat, and this kind of fat is what the brain and the neurons use for insulation. These fats are good because they increase the speed of nerve impulses and connections. Omega-3 fats also combat depression, enhance learning and memory, and serve as major aids to brain plasticity (recreating brain structures for efficiency of neuron transmission).

Not all fish produce needed quantities of omega-3 fats, so this table provides options that fulfill the quantity requirements.

Foods Containing Omegas

Sardines
Mackerel
Salmon
Herring
Blue fish tuna
Lake trout
Flax seeds
Walnuts
Soybeans
Raw Tofu
Winter Squash
Cauliflower
Cabbage
Mustard Seed
Kale
Collard greens
Brussels sprouts
Turnip greens
Shrimp
Strawberries

Folic acid – This nutrient is one of three B-Complex vitamins you can buy. Folic acid as well as Vitamin 6 and 12 can be bought in most health food stores. It also can be obtained from dark-green leafy vegetables, lima beans, cauliflower, beef, eggs, and nuts.

Thiamine (Vitamin B1) – This substance helps manufacture acetylcholine, one of the brain's major messengers. It triggers a metabolic process that helps the brain more effectively use the food available to it. Even if you eat only "healthy" food, if it lacks B1 there is little gain. Nuts and whole grains are stockpiles of this substance.

Strategic Nutritional Plan for Cognitive Connections

The substances and supplements I've listed are recommended for general mental improvement. These supplements can tune your brain to enhance brain power and improve the brain's inter-connections of neurons discussed in chapter two.

Food, in addition to air, is the fuel we use for our brains to develop and work efficiently. If we use the metaphor of the automobile engine for our brain, and gasoline and air as metaphors for the food and air we consume, it becomes easy to grasp why we want to use the best possible fuels to make our engines run optimally. The autistic brain is by definition in a developmental surge, and it requires the best fuel we can provide it.

The Autism Answer

Athletes have known this for generations and eat only the best foods for their bodies and minds. Your child is in training in brain development, so be sure to feed him the right foods in order to enhance his performance and abilities.

Reference Sources

Lawlis, Frank, (2008) The Brain Power Cookbook, Plume: New York
Robinson, Maggie, (2003), 20/20 Thinking, Penguin: New York, 2003
Lawlis, Frank, (2006) The IQ Answer, Viking: New York

The Autism Answer

Chapter Six

Skeletal Evaluation for Autism

One of our consistent findings is that children with autistic behaviors show a sudden brain growth spurt around the age of two, which far surpasses their peers. This finding may be related to abnormal levels of serotonin or other neurotransmitters in the brain, which while accelerating intellectual abilities, may also create hyper-arousal in other areas, such as in the emotional centers of the brain. Most intriguing of all is the possibility that this growth may also create an overcrowding, which may cause a negative reaction to the brain or spinal cord.

This is something to think about because congestion can create heat, and when that happens the body senses invasion and disease. This triggers the immune system, and when it finds nothing foreign to destroy, it may potentially turn to the developing brain and inadvertently begin destroying healthy cells.

This would help explain some other findings (to be discussed later), but it is very interesting that craniosacral manipulation has been shown to help the behavior of these individuals. Craniosacral manipulation involves working with the spine and the skull and its cranial sutures, diaphragms, and fascia. This suggests that autism could result from the disruption of normal brain development in early fetal stages which may be caused by defects in genes that control brain growth and that regulate how neurons communicate with each other.

The congestion around the spinal cord outlets in the neck might also be an important consideration while looking at brain issues. The neck vertebras may not be shifted as much as they are twisted or in a position that creates tension. Consider the mechanical illustration:

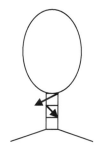

Muscle tension can also be tested using EMG (Electromyography) measurements indicating that the stress may be induced due to the muscular imbalance as well. It seems logical that such an imbalance would also create problems with spinal fluid processes and increased pressures.

Behaviors to look for associated with muscle tension

- Children who have this tension-associated neurology problem often have headaches or stomach pain and discomfort, especially when they are stressed.

The Autism Answer

- Children with craniosacral problems also have problems with balance and visional coordination.
- Children's postures may be affected by this problem.

The Autism Answer

Evaluation and Treatment

According to the medical literature, the problems that result from a restriction in this area affect four main components: arterial blood, capillary blood (brain volume), venous blood and cerebrospinal fluid (CSF). The explanation for this function is based upon the tension created by the cerebellum and its hemispheres moving in opposite directions, resulting in an increase in pressure which squeezes the third ventricle. The pulsation is a recurrent embryological development of the brain.

Craniosacral therapy (bodywork or therapy) is an alternative medicinal therapy used by osteopaths, massage therapists, naturopaths, chiropractors, and occupational therapists. A craniosacral therapy session involves the therapist placing their hands on the patient, which they say allows them to tune into what they call the craniosacral system. The practitioner gently works with the spine and the skull and its cranial sutures, diaphragms, and muscles. In this way, the restrictions of nerve passages are said to be eased, the movement of cerebrospinal fluid through the spinal cord is said to be optimized, and misaligned bones are said to be restored to their proper position.

A typical craniosacral therapy session is performed with the client fully-clothed, in a supine position, (lying down) and usually lasts about one hour. A ten-step protocol serves as a general guideline, which includes (1) analyzing the base (existing) cranial rhythm, (2) creating a still point in that rhythm at the base of the skull, (3) rocking the sacrum, (4) lengthening the spine in the lumbar-sacral region, (5) addressing the pelvic, respiratory and thoracic diaphragms, (6) releasing the hyoid bone in the throat, and (7-10) addressing each one of the cranial bones.

The practitioner may use discretion in which steps are suitable for each client, and may or may not follow them in sequential order, with time restraints and the extent of trauma being factors. Patients often report a sense of deep relaxation during and after the treatment session, and may feel light-headed. This is popularly associated with increases in endorphins (internal pain transmitters). There are few reports of adverse side effects from CST treatment.

Results to look for:
- Better coordination
- Less stressful behavior
- Improved Vision and other sensory integration
- Easier verbal articulation
- Greater efficiency with other treatments

Reference Sources

Pick, Marc, (2003) Cranial Sutures, Eastland Press: Vista, Ca
Upledger, John (2003), Craniosacral Therapy Eastland Press: Vista, Ca

The Autism Answer

Part II

Chapter Seven

Stress

The most frequent issue that brings parents into my clinic is the frustration that comes from lack of control of their children's behaviors, especially when they are throwing a tantrum. They try to discipline with punishment and shame, but they report it only makes it worse. What really places them in conflict is when their child demonstrates this undesirable behavior when they are in public.

The embarrassment and lack of control usually forces them to relent to the demands of the child, which complicates things even further. The fear gains momentum. You fear that you will never understand your child and these behavioral episodes will only gain in force and potentially hurt someone as they grow older and stronger. In losing control, thoughts of institutionalization often follow.

It is sad that there is such misunderstanding of the child and the frustration they are experiencing. There are two main reasons autistic children throw "tantrums." They are either in pain or frightened. Because their sensory systems are so imbalanced, sounds and lights often injure their sensitivities. The sounds in a Wal-mart may not even be in your awareness but they may be screaming in your child's ears like fingernails scraping against a blackboard. The

The Autism Answer

lights may seem so bright to your child that it would compare to search lights beaming directly into your eyes from a few feet away. Their clothes may feel to them like rough sandpaper, such that it is torturous for them to walk.

Their heightened and exaggerated sensory experiences often add to their fears associated with novel and unplanned experiences. This functions to frighten children with autism into having tantrums. The child with autism is constantly stressed due to the incessant demands for re-orientation to their surroundings and the responses by others. A situation can become overwhelming to their sensibilities, and they have not been given the proper training on how to deal with the levels of stress they often experience.

Of all the research and efforts being made to help the autistic challenges, there are no efforts to study ways of helping the autistic child with stress. Yet stress is precisely the problem they need help with most. It is the problem that they face each and every day of their fragile lives and leads to their greatest frustrations.

No child knows what to do intuitively in intensely stressful situations, and one with autism has even less of a chance of coping with stresses. Punishment and blaming only make it worse, making a parent feel powerless and frustrated. This is because so many parents have not been taught the skills necessary to manage stress. Therefore, problems increase with no end in sight.

The Autism Answer

The answers lie in the abilities of the parents to acknowledge these problems and help themselves and their child find ways of stress management. In other words, all the family needs to find are ways to gear down the stress reactions. This process takes coaching and training. This challenge becomes the greatest single possibility for creating an environment in which the child may develop his other skills and abilities for success while also giving the entire family a chance to experience life in a peaceful, happy and meaningful way. We have developed an audio program which I recommend, The MindBody Relaxation Series available at www.MindBodySeries.com/relax, for parents interested in learning highly effective stress management techniques.

Awareness of stress in the child

There are specific clues and behaviors that can help parents become aware of when the child is building up stress. Here are some that might be helpful for observation:

1. The child's breathing becomes rapid or slows to only a slight exchange of air.
2. The child's muscles become tense, especially the shoulders and neck.
3. The child's behavior tends toward escape.
4. The child may not be able to be able to discern where the stressor is coming from, and may react to the person next to him.
5. The child may begin to talk to himself.
6. The child may withdraw.

7. The child may begin to rock or start focusing on his fingers moving
8. The child may start to talk loudly.
9. The child may try to hold onto the wall or retreat into a corner.
10. The child may try to run, not particularly in one direction, but darting here and there because of the tension.
11. The child may begin to try and get more attention since those actions have worked before.
12. The child may start focusing on parts of his body, even masturbating, as ways of dealing with the stress and pain.

There are a number of behaviors the child develops as stress responses, and it would be helpful to recognize them quickly in order to start de-stress training. If the child is in pain, removal from the situation may be the best way of dealing with the problem behavior, not as a punishment but as an avoidance of sensory pain.

The Psycho-Physiological Profile of Stress

Since very few children (or adults for that matter) can articulate what their stresses are, a mental health professional with expertise with children can be helpful. The assessment would be direct and indirect. Also a nonverbal approach would be used, referred to as a Psycho-Physiological Profile.

The direct interview dealing with the history of stress would involve some memories of how certain responses may have been learned. For example, if the child remembers being taken to a place where the sounds were terribly painful, then any return to that place would continue to be stressful. This set of stressors could provide a set of situations to be avoided or situations in which stress management techniques need to be applied.

The indirect approach would be done with alternate methods of communication, such as using drawings, playing with clay, imagination, role-play, and story-telling. The indirect method might also reveal some deep seated anxieties that could be resolved.

The non-verbal methods make use of devices to help the body describe the stress responses. For example, the heart beats faster when the child is stressed, so a pulse meter might be helpful in showing stressful reactions. The blood vessels also tend to shrink when stressed, so the temperature of the fingers and hands will typically correlate to the loss of heat by lack of blood flow, which also can be used to determine the onset of stress. A handy tool to use for this purpose is a finger temperature measurement device. Since these devices are attached to the fingers and cause no pain, these have been frequently used for children.

Other devices often used include a muscle tension device (called an EMG) and a skin conductance device (called a GSR or EDR). They are also attached by small bud-like buttons that use adhesive to adhere to the skin. Breathing rate is also very helpful in assessing stress.

The Autism Answer

One possibility with exciting potential is the ability to use a monitoring program so that the child (and parent) may view the physical responses. This can facilitate therapeutic stress management training. For example, the child might discover that certain breathing patterns reduce his or her heart rate or muscle tension. He might be able to become directly aware of this relationship, and the devices serve to reinforce his ability to mitigate the stressful situations. There are even games a child may learn to lower his stress levels and create constructive stress management techniques for life.

Potential Treatment Choices for Stress Management

The good news is that there are many ways stress management can be taught and many techniques work; however, it is very important to note that too many choices can create stress as well. Find one that works and two backups. Here are some recommendations that have worked well for many of our patients. I might add that parents need techniques as well and it may not always be the case that what works for you works for your child.

Experiment with these techniques with both yourself and your child to find the ones that work best. Try to enjoy the process, rather than creating more stress in your life by worrying too much about which one will work the best. You will notice that it is working if you or your child become more relaxed, as that is the goal of de-stressing.

The Autism Answer

Breathing patterns – There are at least six major breathing patterns that work successfully with autistic children and their parents. Long, slow breaths, especially with emphasis on the out-breath are my favorite to teach. We use a device called the EmWave that is especially successful because its computer customizes a breathing pattern based on the stress level depicted by each person's heart rate variability or steadiness. You may even reinforce the points you that work the best. You may try counting to seven as you breathe in and then count back down to one as you breathe out.

Music – There are numerous music works that help people relax, which has been true since King Sol had David play the harp to sleep. Studies have been done with the works of Mozart and children that show great promise. Lullabies and softly sung songs are great. Even drumming patterns have a major impact on stress. Again, experiment with yourself and your child to find music choices that help to ease your mood and relax. Use the MindBodySeries Autism Audio Program at www.MindBodySeries.com/autismseries as a starting place.

Biofeedback – This therapy uses a kind of technology that helps people train their bodies to release stress. You can find a biofeedback therapist in your area on the website www.bcia.org.

Counseling – These tools can help resolve stressful issues, especially with family problems.

The Autism Answer

Exercise – One of the most effective techniques for de-stressing is exercise, especially rhythmic exercises like dancing and yoga.

Touch therapy – Touch can be a very powerful way of de-stressing a person, but beware as it may also be stress-provoking. This can be a natural extension of care or a carefully considered gesture.

Singing – With virtues related to breathing, singing and humming may be very useful, particularly with regard to releasing emotion.

Talking aloud – Talking about stress and ways of dealing with it can be very helpful, specifically for children.

Praying – If praying means to be still and listen for spiritual guidance, then this can be very meaningful and helpful.

Summary of Thoughts

As this chapter began, the point was emphasized that stress is likely the most significant concern for children with autism, yet the least recognized. If the family can find ways to de-stress the child and themselves, they will find their lives changed immediately for the better – creating greater success in maintaining peace, happiness and comfort in all areas of their lives. Not only will the child advance much quicker in achieving success, there will be greater opportunity to share much needed love and affection.

Reference Sources

The Autism Answer

Campbell, Don, (2002) The Mozart Effect for Children, Harper-Collins: New York
Lawlis, Frank, (2006) The Stress Answer, Viking: New York

Chapter Eight

Sensory Integration Processing Dysfunction

As I discussed earlier, one of the consistent findings of brain mapping and revelations that arise from manual testing, is sensory integration problems. The sensory system is not working together, which means that the information we get from our senses (vision, hearing, touch, smell, and taste) are not balanced either with themselves or with each other.

As explained in the earlier chapter on vision, if you have more than one way of getting information by a sense, such as having two eyes or two ears, there is a strong likelihood that they will be at odds with each other in the case of a child with autism. The right eye will not coordinate with the left eye and the child may be seeing double or their orientation of focus may be confusing. Their left hearing range and information processing may be substantively different than their right.

The Autism Answer

Their senses may not be coordinated with each other so they will see actions that will connect with their hearing, for example. Their touch might be disconnected from the voices or actions they see, making it difficult to watch a person talking to them while listening at the same time.

Their visional perception of their world may not relate to the how they feel with respect to their sense of balance. They may walk very slowly and deliberately as if they are on a rocking ship.

What to look for at home

The following is a checklist that covers several senses that might not have integration. There is likely more than one area that needs training by a professional.

Tactile Sensory Integration Dysfunction

- Your child has difficulty with fine motor tasks such as buttoning, zipping, and fastening clothes.
- Your child may not be able to identify which part of their body was touched if they are not looking.
- Your child may have difficulty using scissors, crayons, or silverware.
- Your child may continue to mouth objects to explore them even after age two.
- Your child has difficulty figuring out physical characteristics of objects; shape, size, texture, temperature, weight, etc.

The Autism Answer

- Your child may not be able to identify objects by feel.

Movement Sensory Dysfunction

- Your child may avoid/dislike playground equipment on which he is apt to lose his balance; i.e., swings or merry-go-rounds
- Your child may prefer sedentary tasks, moves slowly and cautiously, avoids taking risks.
- Your child may physically cling to someone bigger they trust.
- Your child may be afraid of low heights, even the height of a curb or step.
- Your child may be fearful of their feet leaving the ground.
- Your child may be fearful of, and have difficulty riding a bike, jumping, hopping, or balancing on one foot (particularly if his eyes are closed).
- Your child may avoid rapid or rotating movements.

Auditory Sensory Dysfunction

- Your child may be distracted by sounds not normally noticed by others; i.e., humming of lights, fans, or clocks ticking.
- Your child may be distracted and fearful of sounds which he is unclear of their origin or which he does not expect (flushing toilet, hairdryer, squeaky shoes, or a dog barking).
- Your child may refuse to go to movie theaters, parades, skating rinks, musical concerts etc. after a stressful introductory experience.

The Autism Answer

- Your child may decide whether they like or dislike certain people by the sound of their voices.

Oral Sensory Dysfunction

- Your child may be a picky eater, often with extreme food preferences.
- Your child may have difficulty with sucking, chewing, and swallowing; may choke or have a fear of choking.
- Your child may avoid seasoned, spicy, sweet, sour or salty foods; prefers bland foods.

Smell Sensory Dysfunction

- Your child may react negatively to, or dislikes smells that rarely get noticed by other people.
- Your child may tell other people (or talks about) how bad or funny they smell.
- Your child may become bothered/irritated by smell of perfume or cologne.
- Your child may refuse to play at someone's house because of the way it smells.
- Your child may decide whether he likes someone by the way that person smells.

Visual Integration Dysfunction

- Your child may be sensitive to bright lights; will squint, cover eyes, cry and/or get headaches from the light.

The Autism Answer

- Your child may have difficulty keeping eyes focused on task/activity he is working on for an appropriate amount of time.
- Your child may be easily distracted by other visual characteristics (e.g., color, intensity).
- Your child may rub his/her eyes, has watery eyes or gets headaches after reading or watching movies or TV.
- Your child may avoid eye contact.
- Your child may prefer to play in the dark.
- Your child may have difficulty telling the difference between similar printed letters or figures.
- Your child may have a hard time seeing patterns or details within a picture.
- Your child may have difficulty locating small items among other items.
- Your child may have difficulty controlling eye movement to track and follow moving objects.
- Your child may have difficulty telling the difference between different colors, shapes, and sizes.

Auditory Sensory Dysfunction

- Your child may be unable to locate the source of a sound.
- Your child may have difficulty identifying people's voices.
- Your child may have difficulty discriminating between sounds or words (e.g., "picture" vs. "pitcher").

The Autism Answer

- Your child may have difficulty filtering out other sounds while trying to pay attention to one person talking.
- Your child may be bothered by loud, sudden, or high-pitched sounds.
- Your child may have difficulty attending to, understanding, and remembering what is said or read; often asks for directions to be repeated.

Getting Help

It is important to realize that help for your child may be far beyond any parent's understanding of what to do. That is the time to call a professional for help. Please understand that although sensory integration development is a relatively normal process that comes naturally for most children, it has to be taught to the child with autism. But there is good news, because these are teachable processes that have success that may be achieved. There are also tools that may be taught both in facilities and in the home. The parents and family have to be part of the solution, and if done with a positive attitude, they can bring the family closer to one another.

Evaluation and Therapy for Children Age Birth to Three

If your child is under the age of three, you can get a free evaluation through your state's early intervention (EI) program. These programs are federally funded and go by many different names, such as "Birth to Three" or "Child Find." You'll find a full listing of contact numbers for EI programs by state on the website www.sensorysmarts.com.

If your child qualifies for services, EI will provide them for free or for low cost, depending on your state's program. Usually, the therapy sessions will take place in your home, or less often, in an early intervention center-based program. While they are in EI, your child's therapy will focus on everyday life activities, such as playing, doing puzzles, running and jumping, holding a crayon and coloring, dressing, and eating. The document outlining therapy goals and services is called an IFSP, or Individualized Family Service Plan. When your child "ages out" of EI around her third birthday, your service coordinator will help you transition to services supplied by your local school system or community.

Evaluation and Therapy for Children over Age Three

Once your child reaches age three, he is no longer eligible for EI, but can get an OT (Occupational Therapy) evaluation through the school system. Whether your child is three years old and not yet in preschool or age thirteen and attending junior high, your local school district is required to evaluate your child for developmental delays. You can call the special education director at your local school district and ask to set up an evaluation. If your child is found to be eligible for services, he will get an IEP, or individualized education plan. Should "related services" such as OT be recommended after evaluation, the school district is mandated by law to provide therapy.

Professional help: An occupational therapist is usually the primary professional for treating SI dysfunction. However, your child may also be evaluated by a speech-language pathologist, special educator, and often, a physical therapist, in addition to an occupational therapist.

Summary of Thoughts

If you have the opportunity to observe a therapist working with your child, you can begin to appreciate the strategy in sensory skill development. What they are doing most of the time is finding the underlying sensory connections and building the coordination and neural framework from there.

The underlying framework is the fascinating part of this therapy. I am sure you will be educated regarding the treatment plan the therapist works out for your child. My example, which may be a bit awkward for explanatory purposes, is as follows. Suppose your child has auditory sensory integration problems and cannot decode what he hears in order to understand the words spoken to him. It is likely that your child's underlying sensory system lacks the communicative abilities necessary to hear the words as the clustering of syllables or your child may have no visual connection to the words. The therapist might use repetition to link the auditory and visual sensory systems, especially if the child is more of a visual learner. The development pace will vary according to the speed by which your child's brain begins integrating these new skills.

Sensory integration is a vital part of the work done with children diagnosed with autism. Your efforts will be justly rewarded. I have seen marvelous results from these efforts.

References Sources

Ayers, J.A. (1979) Sensory integration and the child. Western Psychological Press: Los Angeles
Grandin, Temple, (2006) Thinking in Pictures, Vintage: New York
Miller, L.C., (2006) Sensational Kids: Hope and help for Children withy sensory processing disorder, Putnam: New York

The Autism Answer

Chapter Nine

Talent and Personality

In writing this guide I want to make sure and not make the mistake many people do when they talk about children who have been diagnosed with autism. We often use labels to categorize them instead of remembering that each child is different and should be regarded as a mystery yet to be known. To be sure, children are like buds blossoming more and more every day, yet we do not know where the buds came from.

From the early days of the Greek philosophers, people have been trying to categorize others. There are been some sophisticated attempts and I actually majored in these statistical techniques in my studies of what is known as psychometrics, the system scientists and doctors use for classification of executives and job types. To a certain degree these tests can be very revealing about yourself or someone you are considering for employment. I even had one professor who picked out his future wife using these "personality tests," but I guess he do not know what he really wanted because they divorced a year later. As you can see, these labels are often misunderstood and frankly, wrong in many cases.

The Autism Answer

The question will always arise: what kind of child is in that body? The quick answer is that there are two sets of descriptions: stable and variable. Stable descriptions are factors that do not change much throughout a lifetime. Some of those are:

People oriented
Focused on tasks
Emotionally sensitive
Intellectually curious
Nervous
Leader/follower
Long term focused
High social value
High material oriented
Dominant/ submissive
Suspicious/trusting
Dependable / not dependable
Group ruled / independent
Practical

The Autism Answer

The variable traits can change quickly and are considered unreliable to be considered as consistent traits. These would be considered to be more emotional reactions or the capacities of a particular person rather than a character profile. Such descriptions might include:

Angry
Sad
Happy
Funny
Anxious
Careful
Attentive
Mad
Frightened
Hurt

As you can see, all of these words can be seen as a range. You can be very hurt or frightened or just a little hurt or frightened. Few people are found to be completely at one end of the spectrum or the other. It is the degree of each that makes us unique and special. There is nothing that is bad or good about our self descriptions; they are only ways of describing how different we can be.

This talent and personality chapter focuses on a very important piece of the assessment in a child who has been diagnosed with autism. They need to be seen and described in their special unique way, so as to remove the trappings of labels. The descriptions may be temporary or stable, but each child yearns to be known as something besides "the autistic kid."

Labels are very limiting and the most important thing about raising a child is to never limit their potential by labeling them. If a child is given a label with limits, there is a tendency to live up to that label. If the parent says to a child, "you are never going to amount to anything," although that statement may be said in a fit of anger, it is nevertheless a sentence by the most important person in that child's life that tells them that none of their goals will ever be reached or that the goals will be so low that they will not be valued. This can be debilitating to the child.

I suspect that most parents know this principle to be true of themselves as well as their children, but what I find is that medical terms have the same limitations. More importantly, the attitude of limiting our expectation and hopes is pervasive to how a child approaches life.

I was pronounced dead at birth, due to the fact that the birth process limited my breathing and no heart beat was found. However, as can be seen, I lived, but the doctor diagnosed me as severely brain damaged and likely mentally retarded. He cautioned my parents to never expect much from me.

The lucky thing about this story is that they never told me the story until I was 14. I had the idea that I could try anything, and even if I failed, it would be a learning experience. That is still my attitude in life, and I have had quite a life, trying out everything I could. I was encouraged to try whatever I thought I could do, and

The Autism Answer

that was a priceless gift my parents gave me. It is the gift you need to give every child, even children with autism. You will be amazed at how amazing they will be.

Talent Search

Probably the most important power you can give a child is to know and support his or her talents. For a child diagnosed with autism, it will be this special talent that will guide them to learn other things. Below are listed some talents these children may possess:

Art
Music
Mathematics
Logic in solving problems
Caring for an animal
Making things with their hands
Designing things
Puzzles
Logical arguments
Composing stories
Sports facts
Sports equipment
Sail boat design

The list can go on indefinitely, but the job of a parent is to help the child discover a talent that they can embrace with passion. You can help them by encouraging them and pointing out to them their successes. Every small success leads to another, therefore the more positive encouragement you can provide, the better. Autistic children like to focus on one or two things and disregard everything else. One child may focus on airplane construction and blow off arithmetic or language skills. By knowing the talent, everything can be geared to support the talent. The mathematics can be based on wing span or travel speed calculations. The language skills can be based on stories about airplanes or people in aviation history.

Talents are important for many reasons. They inspire passion, and they may also involve tools for social contact and interaction. Your child may find a like-minded child to engage in interactions that help them overcome some of their socialization challenges. They could also find self prestige and a special expertise which will allow them the opportunity to enhance their self esteem and self respect. And they can learn what they need to learn by applying this knowledge.

Summary on Talent Assessments

Personality traits and talents are the special arena of psychologists. They have developed many tests and methods to discover these factors, but they have to be appropriate for each person. There are hundreds of tests to choose from that may be applied. Be involved with your child and give him the support he will need in satisfying his personal goals. I promise that you will be amazed.

Psychologists love to find special ways to teach and motivate people. The assessment program may make

The Autism Answer

use of interesting methods to find your child's special aspects of his personality, but the most common methods are having the child draw, interviewing the child, and administering tests to determine intelligence, special aptitudes and interests. More often than not, a child will do well except in one area of intellectual performance, and will mistakenly base his conception of his intelligence based upon that one skill. For example, Manny was tested and although he scored very well in general intelligence levels, on most subtests involving seeing the details of visual puzzles, he scored poorly. As a result he discounted his better scores.

It proved to be insightful because with a better explanation and understanding, his self esteem immediately improved and his motivation increased for those tasks he could do well.

Assessment in this realm of autism is important in order to understand where the child currently is developmentally and what is the child's overall potential. Having this knowledge serves to help devise an effective treatment plan. It is always an exciting discovery when you find that special nugget of talent that proves to be the beacon of hope.

Reference Sources

Lawlis, Frank (2008), Mending the Broken Bond, Viking: New York
Lawlis, Frank, (2004) The ADD Answer, Viking: new York

Chapter Ten

Learning Styles

Autistic children are not dumb or crazy. In fact, they are smart, but they do have special learning styles. The big question often arises: Do you put your child with autism in public school or private specialty school? The answer is always based upon how the child learns. We all have specific ways we learn, and as public schools become increasingly geared to a rigid array of topics (and discouraging different learning styles), it is not difficult for a student to get lost and disinterested while in school, especially for a child with autism.

Unfortunately, schools are under high demand for performance in science and hard academics, and the only mode of education seems limited to the 1 teacher to 30 students model – which is a lecture style in use since pre-Colonial times. There is little elasticity or flexibility to create an educational program customized to a student's special needs and specific ways he learns the best.

Parents usually have to take the leadership role in providing vital information about their child and working with the educational facility to exact the maximum benefit for their child. There needs to be an educational profile by which specific realistic goals may be mapped out for success on an individual basis. Educational success may ultimately be the best psychotherapy for a child. By seeing progress and equipping themselves with gains in knowledge and skills, a child's self esteem can soar.

The educational assessment must include aptitudes for various subjects so that the goals are appropriate and have value. If a student is overwhelmed by demands that are too rigorous for his present stage of development, it will only discourage him from trying. On the other hand, if expectations are too low, this will discourage him from giving his full effort.

Strategies for Learning

Although there are many learning styles to be explored, there are two main factors that pertain to what we know about the brain issues discussed earlier: timing and structure. As discussed in sensory processing, the typical processing for an autistic brain is slower than the average pace of a normal brain. The child can learn the same material as the average child, but he has to take the information in at a slower pace, at least in the beginning.

The first factor is timing, which can be thought of as the pace at which they are able to process new information. Think of the autistic brain as having many neurons attempting to attach themselves in clusters that make sense. When a new topic is presented, the process of plugging these connectors together takes longer than it does in a normal brain. This may be due to tangled up visual information, verbal information or a combination of factors.

The Autism Answer

I have a little verbal sensory input slowness. I notice it when people spell out words to me and I find myself having difficulty processing the letters. I usually find myself having to ask three times. Otherwise, I do the same thing many children with autism, I give up. What works is to start slowly, very slowly, and gradually speed up. I imagine more neurons aligning in their brains as they are slowly processing the new information. For example, if you were teaching the word, "mother", you would say it very slowly, emphasizing the syllables, such as MUHHHHHH-THERRRRR. As the child begins repeating the word, the pace may be increased.

This is the way I learn languages. I hear the word such that the syllables are very distinctive and clear. As the sounds become established in my brain, I can begin to recognize the word from a general framework of sounds. And as the recognition becomes easier, there is a pride and joy in learning.

The other critical learning factor that is very often associated with how the autistic brain processes new information is structure. This is essential for knowing how to teach the child with autism. One skill that is very well developed is learning rules. This is due to the fact that it is structure that is the primary "need" of the autistic brain. The unfortunate corollary to this is lack of flexibility and lack of ability to generalize from one situation to another. However, we need to use structure first to build upon their strengths.

Learning Styles

As implied in earlier statements, everyone has preferred learning styles. For the child with an autistic brain, it becomes paramount to utilize their most effective style and teach material within this framework. Although there may be many unique learning styles identified for a child, the five most common learning styles are:

- The visual-learner
- The verbal learner
- The hands-on learner
- The trial-and-error learner
- The cognitive learner

The visual learner is a person who sees pictures and images as the problems in his or her mind. This person prefers art and other visual matters; even scientific architecture may be an interest in their education. They often think and learn visually. Creating visual representations of educational goals would be a major help in maintaining this person's interest and understanding of a subject. For example, imaging words would be better than talking about them.

The verbal learner is one who enjoys listening and creating word problems and stories. Words are intriguing not only in how they sound but also in the complexity of the language itself. Most likely this type of learner is most easily integrated in public schools since the curriculum is geared heavily in this approach.

The Autism Answer

The hands-on learner is a person who likes to make and repair things with his or her hands. He is more of a concrete learner who understands things in real terms, not in abstract theory. The motto is: does it work or not?

The trial-and-error learner is similar to the hands-on learner except that there is little forethought in planning a project. He may have an intuition, but he learns by trying things out. This type of learner is a headache to the public school teacher because it may take several times of trial-and-error before he gets it right. But please don't count this kind of learner out. They have a lot of energy and perseverance.

The cognitive learner is a math teacher's dream. He likes to work in very logical terms and usually enjoys any logical system that may be used to solve problems. He learns in step-by-step principles so that they make sense. The difficulties he experiences often exist when the problems require memorization and rote answers.

The Autism Answer

Summary of Educational Assessment

The process of assessing a child's strengths and challenges is very important to the success of the educational experience. Typically the autistic child is very focused on whatever their interests and aptitudes are. A child with autism is easily discouraged, so there is a great need to understand how they think and what motivates them. Work with your child to discover which ways they learn the best and you will discover just how incredible a child with autism's intellect and ability to learn new things can be.

Reference Sources

Grandin, Temple, (2008) The Way I see It, Future Horizons: Arlington, Tx
Tammet, D. (2007) Born on a Blue Day, Free Press: New York

The Autism Answer

Part III

Chapter Eleven

The Family Assessment

Most of the assessments described in this guide are dedicated to the child with autism, since everything often revolves around them. However, in reality most of the treatment program will involve the whole family. In fact, it probably already does involve the whole family, either directly or directly. One of the saddest chapters in the history of the treatment of autism was when the mother was to blame for everything. They were labeled as the "refrigerator moms" who put what was referred to as "double-bind" demands on a child, converting the brain into a schizophrenic, split-brain. Thankfully research has put this notion out to pasture and we now know that parents' communication styles are not the cause of autism.

While this is a dark era in the history of autism, it is necessary to address, as sensitive as it will be, the reality that in a small number of situations there are family environments in which the skills are not present for the parents to form bonding relationships with their children. This may have numerous reasons ranging from overworked parents who have no parental training to underlying and undiagnosed conditions that affect social bonding. Overly confused and ill-fated parenting skills can lead to mystification and chaos.

The Autism Answer

Parents do not get a manual on raising autistic children. The only guidance is usually the models that were used on them. Not only are these models often wrong, they don't have much to do with raising a child with autism. It is easy to become devastated with the extra time and patience it requires for this process. I would estimate that twenty hours per week is mandatory to equip the child with the extra time it takes, especially in the beginning. As has been pointed out, the anxiety alone demands extra stress management skills for both parent and child.

Having an autistic child often pulls attention away from other members of the family, the spouse and other children. This division can cause major disruptions in the household which only places more stress on the child with autism.

For these and other reasons, a family assessment is usually needed to determine what coaching and parental skills need to be put in place for the welfare of the whole family. Some of these coaching tips will be briefly discussed in this chapter.

The Autism Answer

Communication Styles

There are different communication styles for parents, based in part on how they were raised and what appealed to their needs. I must say that there is not one "best" style for autism. It is the quality of the approach that matters most. Parenting styles have been broken down into three categories; the authoritarian, the democratic and the permissive.

The authoritarian parent is described as the style in which rules are handed down to the child with rigid consequences. While the negative aspects are usually related to lack of individual needs and the "awful" parent is depicted as a monster, a strong and sensitive authoritarian is often most effective with a child with autism because they are in need of structure and set rules.

The democratic parent is usually depicted as the "task-oriented" agenda-based parent who sets objectives external to the relationship, creating a team spirit. As with all parental styles at the extreme, a rigid democratic parent often comes off as cold because of the lack of sensitivity for the child in reverence to the goals. However, a team spirit among the family is a desired quality for a child with autism. Competitiveness and jealousy can make a terrible life and a team spirit places everything in a win-win situation. For example, when the child learns something new, it is a prize for everyone in the family to celebrate because the ownership of the success is shared.

The Autism Answer

The permissive parent is usually described as a parent who makes the world revolve around the child and everything depends on the needs of the child. This is the style in which the parent would give in to the tantrum with the thought that the child must have a need above hers or those around. This may not be the style that is most helpful for a child with autism. There is no reason why an autistic child should have that right. As indicated earlier the child is likely in pain or scared instead of being manipulative, but autistic children, like all children, do learn to get things they want in manipulative ways.

This can be difficult because parents oftentimes feel sorry for their child with autism, and therefore give in to their demands and tantrums. But they do need structure and rules as to how to behave. These approaches need to be taught in very clear ways. However, the sensitivity of the permissive parenting style is greatly desired because this is the way a parent really learns what the child is like.

Special needs for autistic child care

As repeated throughout this guide, the autistic child wants structure, and that means a carefully designed parental plan. The parent needs to know what reinforcement works, and in line with that concept, what the child's currency is. Currency refers to what a child will work for. Cheerios is one of my consistent favorites for children younger than four or five. They are like candy, but they are mostly air and not bad in the nutrition department.

The Autism Answer

Children will rarely fill up on them, and I like them myself, so I can snack along the way. Some children respond to toys, others go for books and DVDs. Music is a big one as well. As they get older the price usually goes up as well – cell phones, clothes, etc.

I teach a 1-2-3 method of direction for children that I learned from the great coaches in sports. The first step is to stop the undesired behavior. You can simply explain that the behavior does not please you as the parent or that the behavior will not get them what they want. For example, if they act out in a tantrum, you can explain that the behavior will not get them what they want and does not please anyone.

The second step is often left out in disciplinary schemes. It is to suggest alternative methods that will succeed, at least two or three so they have a choice.

The third step is to ensure that when the child does behave in a constructive manner, the behavior is reinforced in some fashion. For example, if they act responsibly and learn to negotiate in a workable manner, they not only may get what they want but you might surprise them with extra goodies. Remember the power of positive reinforcement. Children want their parents to be proud of them.

Too often parents just expect their children to know what to do in complex situations, and when they don't, instead of teaching them a better way, they punish them with anger. Everyone loses, no one learns anything different, and the same behavior continues.

The Autism Answer

Every parent should have a set of principles for disciplining that are sound and that work.

Learning Expansion

Autistic children are usually very good in learning rules because this is the structure they function the best in. But they are not so good in the generalization of those rules. For example, they may understand how to "play" with person A, but when person B tries to engage them, they do not know what to do. This expansion of principles will have to be taught. Our communication system is very complex and subtle and it is sometimes hard to understand, even for the average child.

There is confusion when people of different statuses show up and kids do not know the change in rules. You behave differently when Dad's boss comes to dinner. You behave differently when Grandma shows up. You go to a restaurant and everything is different once again, even if you eat the same things. It is bewildering to children, and it is worse for someone who needs to learn these things with very structured methods.

The Autism Answer

Summary

Parenting assessment may be the most important feature of this process, and it should be an integrated part of any treatment plan. Parents have to have support and much consultation for each challenge they face. I always recommend that parents get as many resources as they can. I want them to create a list of people who can help and who they can make part of their parenting plan. It is an exhausting job and can be very frustrating, in fact your frustration with your child will likely pale against the frustration you experience in trying to gain community support and assistance. Schools have to be talked to and medical care has to be managed differently. Your whole life is a learning curve. Reach out for every resource you hear about.

Breakthroughs have been achieved through what has been coined as "mindsight" or emotional sensitivity for both parents and child. This process is guided by learning what emotional states are in experiential terms and learning to mirror behaviors that bring about positive results.

Reference Sources

Chawarska, K., Volkmar, F. (2005) Autism in Infancy and early Childhood. In F. Volkmar, R. Paul, A. Klin & D. J. Cohen (Eds.) Handbook of autism and pervasive developmental disorders (3rd. ed., Vol. 1, pp. 223-246). Wiley: Hoboken

The Autism Answer

Lawlis, Frank, (2007) Mending the Broken Bond, Plume: New York

The Autism Answer

Concluding Remarks

What your child with autism can give you

This guide has been specifically about what assessments you can expect and use for your plan to enhance your child's success and wellbeing in life. However, it is not a one-way street. Your child can benefit you as well. Yes, the life of a parent with an autistic child can be very challenging and is definitely full of emotional roller-coasters. But, there is a positive side to it all that we must not forget.

I promise that you will never see another child with the same determination and effort in life. He comes from a lower stage of development and like in a race, coming from behind takes focus and belief in self. You may become aware that he or she may have more faith than you, and there is an inspiration that comes from being an observer of true grit.

There will be huge spans to jump and many may not be appropriate, but the enduring courage will astound you at times. There will be instances that you, as a parent, will begin to know yourself better as well and the "why me" questions will start to have answers. Life will have that spiritual sense that can never be replaced. And perhaps you may realize that you are one of the luckiest people in the world.

About Dr. Frank Lawlis

Dr. Lawlis has focused on clinical and research methods of the mind-body relationship since 1968 when he received his Ph.D. in Psychology with an emphasis in medical psychology and rehabilitation. He was awarded the Diplomate (A.B.P.P.) in both Counseling Psychology and Clinical Psychology. He also received the status of Fellow from the American Psychological Association for his scientific contributions to the field of clinical psychology and behavioral medicine, as well as other awards for his pioneering research in this field.

Having served on five prestigious medical school faculties in the Departments of Psychiatry, Orthopedic Surgery, and Rehabilitation Medicine and five graduate psychology faculties, he has blazed new studies and approaches in the care of patients with chronic and acute pain, cancer and psychosomatic problems. The Medical Schools attended were New York Medical Center (1967-68), Texas Tech Medical School (1973-75), Universities of Texas Health Center (UTHC) at San Antonio (1975-76), UTHC at Dallas (1979-89) and Stanford Medical School (1991-93).

Dr. Lawlis has authored and co-authored more than 100 articles and chapters as well as four textbooks; Imagery and Disease (IPAT: Champaign, Ill., 1984), Bridges of the Bodymind (IPAT, 1980), Transpersonal Medicine (Shambhala Publ., Boston, 1996), The Mosby Textbook on Alternative Medicine (Mosby, 2001), The ADD Answer, The IQ Answer, Mending The Broken Bond, The Stress Answer and, most recently, The Brain Power Cookbook. In addition to his literature, Dr. Lawlis has published audio works available at MindBodySeries. Dr. Lawlis has developed programs for Anxiety, PTSD, Depression, Sleep,

ADD/ADHD and Creativity and demonstrated them on the Dr. Phil Show.

Dr. Frank Lawlis cofounded the <u>Lawlis and Peavey PsychoNeuroPlasticity Center</u> in Lewisville Texas as a new innovation for psychological assessment wherein an individual would have a thorough medical-psychological-neurological-sociological-family dynamics evaluations during the same week. With the intensive focus approach, the multilayers of interactions can be addressed quickly and with less frustration and discouragement. Moreover, there would be a specific plan to redevelop brain functions and coordinate their sequencing such that even major challenges could be overcome within a quicker time frame. Through this process great steps have been taken to understand an individual's problems and to address all the issues during a finite time period.

Dr. Frank Lawlis has been Chief Content and Oversite Adviser as well as Chairman of the Dr. Phil Advisory Board and Member of the Dr. Phil and Robin Foundation since the inception of the show. He is responsible for evaluating potential show themes and guests to determine benefit of  the concepts, consulting with Dr. Phil on various guests (often appearing on the shows themselves), and overseeing resources for the guests as they leave the show. Being a major force in the conception of the themes he interacts with every factor in the development with the shows.

Contact Dr. Frank Lawlis
drlawlis@mindbodyseries.com
PNP Center
571 W. Main Street
Suite 210
Lewisville, Texas 75057

www.lawlispeavey.com
www.mindbodyseries.com
www.youthapedia.com

33497062R10072